Carry Aylward

NUTSHELL BOOKS

www.nutshell-books.com

ISBN: 978-1-8384748-4-3

Front cover design by Nutshell Books
Book design by Nutshell Books
Photography: © AdobeStock,
© Shutterstock, © iStock

Printed by Kindle Direct Publishing

First printed 2022

Nutshell Books
3 Holmlea Road, Goring on Thames
RG8 9EX, United Kingdom
www.nutshell-books.com

This book is dedicated to you, the reader,
for wanting to be an excellent owner,
and for the super-special Cavalier King
Charles Spaniel you bring into your
heart and home

CONTENTS

FOREWORD

Whether you've already brought your gorgeous bundle of puppiness into your home, or you're still weighing up the pros and cons of owning a Cavalier King Charles Spaniel, this is a hugely exciting time. And I'm thrilled for you because this is the sweetest, gentlest and most empathetic of breeds.

Responsibly-bred and well-raised, these dogs don't have a bad bone in their bodies. And they're as comfortable in their own silky coats as they are with the world at large.

They're also extremely tactile and want little more than to cuddle and be cuddled. Like living lap warmers, they will drape their long-eared silky-soft selves over you at every opportunity.

There's little doubt your precious puppy will render you loopy with love, but there will also be times when a Cavalier will leave you fraught with frustration. As a breed they love to be the centre of attention, the result of this being that they can be very easily mollycoddled. They can sulk like spoilt children when told off; they will mope if they feel they're being ignored; and they don't respond well to harsh voices or rough treatment of any sort.

But whether or not you've owned one before, you've chosen the perfect starter guide for Cavalier puppy parents-to-be.

In the chapters that follow, we will look at the traits and characteristics most typical of the Cavalier King Charles; the joys and challenges you are likely to encounter in the breed; and how best to manage your new puppy-homelife balance. You will be led step by step through the entire process, from deciding whether a Cavalier is a good choice for you, through the first days, to the subsequent weeks and months – the all-important formative time when your puppy is growing and learning at its fastest, and when you need to put the most energy into its upbringing and training.

If it turns out that the Cavalier you choose is one of the increasingly popular Cavalier mixes, like the Cavapoo or Cavoodle, most of the tips and advice in these pages will still be useful. It will give you an appreciation of the Cavalier side of your dog's ancestry and help you to be a more understanding owner.

Because 'Cavalier King Charles Spaniel' is such a mouthful, the breed will usually be referred to in a shortened form such as 'Cavalier King Charles', 'Cavalier', or even just 'Cavvie'.

Also for the sake of easy reading, at times your puppy will be referred to as 'he' and at other times as 'she', but please consider both 'he' and 'she' to mean 'he or she' in every suitable instance.

I sincerely hope the advice that follows will help you to build a solid foundation for a wonderful relationship with your Cavalier. May it keep you smiling – not only through the love and cuddles, but also through the puddles and poops, heart-wrenching nights, and shredded items of value.

For now, brace yourself with unconditional love and a good sense of humour, and let's get started.

1. ARE YOU READY?

If you're undecided about a puppy, and specifically a Cavalier King Charles Spaniel, this chapter will help you to make a more informed decision.

Cavaliers have kind and gentle natures which make them a good choice for most people, including the elderly, small children and first-time dog owners. They make truly wonderful companions. But before we delve into the specifics of their characteristics, and how to raise and care for a Cavalier, let's run through some quick but important questions. Because choosing a dog is a momentous, life-changing and long-term decision.

If you are new to owning a dog, any dog, when you invite one into your world, your life will never be the same. You will soon start thinking differently about what you wear, the places you visit, your holiday destinations and possibly even the car you drive. Your life will also be warmer, messier, happier and richer in so many ways.

But are you really ready for a dog?

If you invite a dog into your home, it should be treated like family. Ask yourself very honestly whether, at this time in your life, and for the next ten to 15 years in the case of a Cavalier, you will be able to give it the love, care, time, exercise, training and patience it deserves. No dog should ever be cast aside because its owner has grown tired of the responsibility.

Is a puppy right for you?

Ask yourself honestly whether you can face the puppy stage with the pooping, weeing and chewing of everything in sight. An adolescent Cavalier can be a handful – right until around two years of age – and needs a great deal of training and socialising. Ask yourself whether you have the time and energy. If not, you might consider taking on an older dog. An adult that needs re-homing will have finished with toilet training, teething and even adolescence.

You could contact an established and reputable breeder to find out about giving an ex-breeding dog the chance to live as a pet. Or you could take on a Cavalier that hasn't performed as well as expected as a therapy dog or in the show ring.

Another option is to give a home to a dog in its senior years. There are so many beautiful older dogs that need re-homing through no fault of their own, so if you're no longer as strong or active as you once were, this might be the best choice for you now.

Do you have other pets?

If you choose a Cavalier, especially as a puppy, there's no reason for it to have any problems with your existing pets – dogs and cats in particular. But your existing pets mightn't be quite so adaptable. Think carefully how they might react to their new family member.

You still want a puppy?

I know. They're warm and cuddly and there's nothing as sweet as the pitter patter of puppy feet. But a puppy is a big investment – financially as well as in terms of time, energy and emotion.

This is not an attempt to put you off getting a dog. It's just important that you are sure you are able to give your puppy the happy life it deserves and fully understand the commitment you're making. Too many dogs are re-homed and even euthanised each year because their owners underestimated the responsibility.

Also, be sure to involve any other members of the household in this decision. The more say the family has had from the start in owning a dog, choosing the breed, and choosing your specific puppy, the more likely they will be to actively engage with and care for it, and the less likely they'll be to shirk their dog-walking, poo-picking responsibilities.

Now if you're still sure a puppy is the way forward, and you're brave enough to let those four extra feet into your heart and home, then let's take a closer look at the Cavalier King Charles Spaniel.

WHY CHOOSE A CAVALIER?

Wherever you are in your puppy-finding journey, and even if you've already brought your special puppy home, it's useful to know the traits and characteristics you'll encounter in the breed. These are not necessarily good or bad in themselves, they are simply more or less right for you and your circumstances.

Temperament

This is one of the main reasons people choose a Cavalier. They're about as sweet as can be. Well-raised, they are:

- gentle, sensitive and empathetic
- eager to please and natural pleasers
- friendly with everyone
- happy-go-lucky
- infinitely patient with children
- playful and fun-loving

- funny and cheeky
- loyal and devoted to their owners
- forgiving.

They can sometimes be stubborn, or a little reserved in new company, but no breed is perfect.

Adaptable

Whether you're an experienced dog owner or this is a new experience for you, Cavaliers make ideal family companions. With their friendly, easygoing natures, they get along with everyone and everything. They're good with small children and the elderly, with other dogs and most other pets. And unlike some breeds, they form strong bonds with the whole human family, and not just one person.

By way of exercise, they're just as happy walking with you for hours as they are snuggling up with you on the sofa all day. This is because they have enough ancestry from the Sporting Group of dogs to be playful and energetic, and enough qualities from the Toy Group of dogs to be perfectly content staying quietly indoors. (We will look at dog groups in the next chapter.)

Their caring natures make them good therapy and assistance dogs, they excel in the show ring, and are good in obedience as well as agility classes.

Comforters

Cavaliers love physical contact. Given the choice, they'll be right by your side day and night. They'll follow you from room to room, and jump on your lap at every opportunity. Then they'll drape themselves over you like an expensive throw. They are comfort-loving creatures and natural lapdogs.

Lookers

Cavalier King Charles Spaniels look every bit as regal as their 'title' suggests. Hallmarks of the breed are the gentle expression, round engaging eyes, long dangly ears and silky-smooth coat. They are stately dogs that carry themselves with grace and poise.

A good size

They're an ideal size for a household companion, averaging 30.5-33cm (12-13") in height at the withers, and weighing between 5.4 and 8.2kg (12-18lb) when fully grown.

Need exercise

Cavaliers need less physical exercise than average breed, but they do still need a good hour a day. If this will be too much for you, you might want to consider a small breed with no Sporting ancestry.

Cavs need mental exercise too. Training and games that provide mental stimulation are just as essential to keep them happy and well-balanced. And the more things you give them to do and to play with, the less likely they'll be to find things on their own – things that might involve redecorating the furniture for instance.

Need company

Cavvies are highly prone to separation anxiety. They're very sociable dogs and will easily become depressed or miserable if left alone for long stretches. Don't get one if you're going to be out at work all day.

Attention-seekers that need careful management

Cavaliers can be demanding – they love to be the focus of attention, which can be incredibly sweet, especially in a puppy. But this trait needs to be kept in check or you could find yourself with an attention-seeking companion that's ruling your life. And yet, when their attention-seeking turns to pestering, you can't be too hard on them because harsh voices can lead to neurotic responses. In fact rough treatment of any sort can cause them great stress and even depression. So there's a delicate balance to be found here, which makes it all the more important that you, and all the members of your household, don't spoil your puppy. You need to be consistently and quietly firm but fair. There's plenty of advice coming up on this.

Need grooming

Cavaliers are generally clean dogs, but they ALL shed, and many enjoy getting wet and muddy. They're not a good choice for the super house-proud.

They are also pretty high maintenance when it comes to grooming. Their long silky coats need regular brushing – anything from daily to twice a week – to keep them clean and matt-free. Their floppy ears need regular checking and cleaning and, like all the Toy breeds, their teeth should be cleaned regularly too.

Training

Cavaliers are considered of average intelligence, but their eagerness to please is a great advantage in obedience training. By nature, your puppy will want to please you, so the odds are already tipped in your favour.

However they're not known to be quick with toilet (potty) training.

They can also be proper little escape artist, who then have little to no road sense. If you have a garden or yard, be sure to plug every gap before bringing your puppy home.

Not good as guard dogs or watch dogs

Cavaliers are not aggressive so they'd be no good as guard dogs. Some Cavaliers might pass as watchdogs, barking when there's someone at the door, but as soon as that door's opened they will most likely welcome the person with tail-wagging delight. They're simply too friendly.

Weak strains and traits

Cavaliers are prone to a number of health issues, the most common of which is inherited heart disease. But you can significantly minimise the risk of genetic health problems by choosing a puppy bred from parents with the recommended health clearance certificates. (See 'Buying responsibly' in Chapter 3.)

Cost

A good puppy from fully-health-tested parents is not cheap, and after buying your puppy, the cost of pet insurance, vets' bills, food, toys and care is no small consideration.

Bottom line

As with all breeds, if Cavaliers' needs are not met – if they are left alone or locked up for long stretches for example – they have the potential to become 'difficult': barking, digging and chewing things.

But all Cavvie puppies have the makings of wonderful pets, so if you can give yours the love, exercise and stimulation it needs, you are about to discover devotion and entertainment beyond measure.

2. WHAT MAKES A 'GOOD' CAVALIER KING CHARLES SPANIEL?

By now I expect you've decided that you do want a Cavalier, and I'm thrilled for you. There are wonderful times ahead. And more love than you could ever imagine.

But don't rush off to see the first litter you come across – even if you want no more from your Cavvie than good company. Why? Because it's close to impossible to resist the pleading eyes of a puppy that wants to go home with you. Once those eyes have found your heart, they are most likely stuck there for life. Better to plan ahead. Start doing your research so you can make a wise and informed choice.

If it's a companion pet you're after, you'll be less particular than someone who's looking for a working dog, show dog or a dog you might be thinking of using for breeding. The puppies could all grow into lovely dogs, but if you don't want to risk weak strains and traits, it's well worth taking the time to track down a litter that is a credit to the breed.

So let's start with that. What is it that makes a Cavalier a Cavalier? And what makes it a 'good' one? The rest of this chapter will give you a basic understanding of the breed, and a feel for what is, and what isn't, considered desirable.

What is a 'true' Cavalier King Charles Spaniel?

If your dog were to be entered into a showing class, she would be judged against the Cavalier King Charles Spaniel breed standard. This is a list of attributes considered to be 'ideal' by the Kennel Club of your country.

Because the standards differ slightly from country to country, you might like to visit the website of your own country's Kennel Club for specific details, but for the purposes of this book, the following is a general summary. Of course your dog needn't tick all these boxes to be a lovely dog, but it's useful and interesting to know what is expected of a well-bred adult Cavalier.

THE BREED STANDARD

Temperament

Sporting and fearless, yet gentle and affectionate. No tendency towards nervousness or aggression.

Physical appearance

- **Overall:** Active, graceful, regal and well-balanced with a sweet, gentle, melting expression
- **Coat:** Long and silky. Can have a slight wave, but must be free from curl. Plenty of feathering (longer hair on ears, chest, legs, tail and feet). No trimming is permitted, apart from the undersides of the feet.
- **Permitted colouring:**
    - **Blenheim:** Rich chestnut markings well broken up on a pearly white ground. Markings on the head to be evenly spaced, with a white blaze between the eyes and ears. A lozenge or

'Blenheim spot' in the centre of the blaze is desirable.
    - **Tricolour:** Black and white markings, well spaced, with tan markings over eyes, on cheeks, inside ears, inside legs and on underside of tail.
    - **Ruby:** A rich red all over.
    - **Black and Tan:** Jet black with rich tan markings over eyes, on cheeks, inside ears, on chest, legs, and underside of tail.
- **Size and proportion:** Adult weight from 5.4-8.2kg (12-18lbs), and proportionate to height. Height ideally 30.5-33cm (12-13") at the withers. Height from withers to elbow equals height from elbow to the ground.
- **Head and neck:** Head proportionate to size of dog. Skull quite flat between high-set ears. Neck slightly arched at the crest.
- **Eyes:** Large and round but not prominent, and set well apart. Dark brown in colour. Rims dark. There should be cushioning under the eyes.
- **Ears:** Set high on the head. Long with plenty of feathering.
- **Muzzle and nose:** Muzzle tapered but not sharp or pointed. Length from base of stop (dividing point between

the muzzle and skull) to tip of nose about 3.8cm (1.5"). Nostrils black, without flesh marks, and well developed.

- **Teeth:** A perfect, regular scissor bite, i.e. the upper teeth closely overlapping the lower teeth and set square into the jaws.
- **Body:** Level back and short-coupled, with ribs well sprung.
- **Legs:** Moderately boned. The hindlegs when viewed from the rear should be parallel from hock to heel. Feet compact, well cushioned and well feathered.
- **Tail:** Well set on, carried happily but never much above the level of the back, and in constant motion when the dog is in action. (Docking is illegal in the UK and optional in the USA, with no more than one third to be removed.)

Movement

Free and elegant with good reach in front, and drive from behind. Forelegs and hindlegs move in parallel when viewed from in front or behind.

'CAVALIER KING CHARLES' v 'KING CHARLES'?

The Cavalier King Charles is one of over 20 breeds of Spaniel. Most of these are reasonably distinctive, but the Cavalier King Charles is often confused with the King Charles, and not just in name. So what is a Cavalier in the dog world, and what is the difference between this and the King Charles? A little bit of background here will put this into context. Let's start by looking at the dog Groups.

Toy Group or Sporting Group?

Kennel Clubs all over the world sort dog breeds into Groups that share broadly defined characteristics. Terriers for example share the hardiness and bravery that makes them good for hunting vermin.

Cavaliers are in the Toy Group of dogs which are bred to be lap-sized companions who are friendly, fun-loving and attention-seeking but don't need huge amounts of exercise. They are the largest breed in the Group and, together with the King Charles, they are the only Spaniels in this Group.

All the other strains of Spaniel are classed in the Sporting (USA) or Gundog (UK) Groups, whose member breeds are energetic, have a strong instinct to retrieve game, and love a challenge.

But not every breed fits perfectly in its category and the Cavalier is in fact a strange mix of Toy and Sporting dog. A quick step back in time will help to make this clearer.

How the breed came about

Spaniels as a whole date back over more than a thousand years, and Toy Spaniels more specifically can be traced to the 16th Century – having most likely been bred down in size from Sporting breeds. Queen Elizabeth I famously had one, as did Mary, Queen of Scots. But it was later, in the courts of Charles I and his son Charles II, that their popularity spread, especially among the nobility.

These Toy Spaniels were selectively bred to be lapdogs for aristocratic ladies. The goal was to breed companion pets that physically resembled the Sporting Spaniels, but were smaller, calmer, gentler, and lacked some of the drive.

The King Charles Spaniel

Then in the 1600s, a number of Pug-like breeds were brought to Europe from East Asia, and these became hugely popular in the Toy breeds. Toy Spaniels were crossbred with these flatter-faced breeds resulting in a new strain that was smaller than the 'original' Toy Spaniel, with a shorter muzzle, larger rounder eyes and more domed heads. In 1903, Edward II of England named this breed the King Charles Spaniel, after King Charles I and II.

The number of 'original' Toy Spaniels – the ones that had been popular before the crossbreeding with flatter-faced dogs – then declined considerably.

The Cavalier in particular

In the early 1900s, however, a group of breeders focused their efforts on its revival. They wanted to revert to the slightly larger Spaniels, with longer muzzles, flatter skulls and stronger sporting instincts. The word 'Cavalier' was chosen to distinguish this type from the flatter-faced King Charles.

In 1928, the first Cavalier King Charles Spaniel Club was formed and in 1945 the Kennel Club recognised the Cavalier as a separate breed from the King Charles.

3. FINDING THE LITTER

DECIDE WHAT YOU'RE LOOKING FOR

With this basic understanding of the breed, you are well placed to begin your search for a litter of good and well-bred puppies. But first you might like to work out some basic preferences. You needn't stick to them, but they'd be useful as a guide.

Purebred or crossbreed

A purebred is a dog whose parents are of the same breed. So if you do want a purebred Cavalier King Charles Spaniel, it is important that you meet the mother, and if it's not possible to meet the father, that you at least get to see photos or video footage of him. This is because many backyard breeders mate their females with other breeds and still advertise the puppies as 'purebreds'. The puppies might grow into lovely dogs, but they are unlikely to have the traits of a true Cavalier King Charles Spaniel.

Coat colour and markings

As we saw in the Breed Standard, there are four official types to choose from. The most popular is the Blenheim with its combination of chestnut and pearly white. Around half of Cavaliers boast this colouring which was developed by the first Duke of Marlborough who lived at Blenheim Palace in Oxfordshire, England. Some of these dogs have a lozenge-shaped mark on the centre of their heads, in the white blaze between the ears. This is known as the 'Blenheim spot' or 'Duchess thumb print' and is considered both lucky and desirable. The story goes that when General John Churchill fought in the Battle of Blenheim, his wife waited anxiously for his return, hugging her pregnant Toy Spaniel for comfort and pressing her thumb to the top of its head. Churchill was victorious and when the puppies arrived, they all had these 'lucky' lozenge marks.

The Tricolour Cavalier, originally called the Prince Charles, is the next most popular colouring for the breed, followed by the Black and Tan, which was originally the King Charles. The Ruby colouring was the last to be developed.

You most likely already have a favourite among these colourings and perhaps you're wondering whether certain colours and markings are typically associated with certain characteristics. With Cavvies there is some talk of the Black and Tans possibly being the most vocal. But apart from that, there is nothing to suggest that a Cavalier's temperament or behaviour can be linked to its colouring. Whatever you choose will be lovely.

Girl or boy?

If you already have another dog, and that dog has been neutered (de-sexed or spayed), it would be sensible to choose a puppy from the opposite sex to avoid jealousy or competition. That said, if your existing dog is un-neutered, a puppy from the opposite sex mightn't be such a good idea.

But other dogs aside – and if you're not hoping to use your puppy for breeding someday – I don't believe there's much in it. Your Cavvie will be incredibly loving whatever it is. Girl or boy, each one really is his or her own 'person', and health and temperament are far more important considerations. Good training and keeping your puppy in its right place in the family 'pack' are much better determining factors in how he or she will turn out.

Neutering, however, **is** a very important consideration. If un-neutered, females will come into heat roughly every six months – which could result in mood swings and aggressiveness towards other females – and there is, of course, the risk of unwanted pregnancy. Both males and females, but males to a greater extent, can adopt unwanted sexual behaviours like urinating to mark their territory.

Neutering can be the answer to these behaviours in both sexes, but we will look at this in more detail in the chapter 'Going forward'.

One or two?

If you're considering more than one Cavvie, it's always better to get one at a time. This is so that you can get a feel for the breed, not to mention the cost and effort required. Even if you already have your heart set on two, it's best not to get them from the same litter. That would prevent the puppies from bonding with you, rather than with each other and, on top of that, behaviour problems with siblings are common.

TIMING

The best time to pick up your puppy

As well as getting an idea of the sort of puppy you're looking for, you need to decide on the best time to bring it home. This should be at the beginning of a stretch when you, or most of the family, will be home and able to care for him full-time for most of the day. If you're retired this mightn't be a consideration, but if you're a working family with school-going children, for example, you should try to pick your puppy up early in the school holidays.

The weather is another consideration. If you live in a country or area where the summer and winter temperatures are very different, or the wet seasons are extreme, then getting your puppy at the start of a warm or dry season will make for easier toilet training.

No puppy of any breed should ever leave its mother and the litter before it is eight weeks old. In fact, the Toy breeds mature later than larger breeds, and the Cavalier King Charles Spaniel Club in the US recommends 10-12 weeks. That is because this is a crucial development stage when puppies are building their immune systems and learning important lessons from their mother and litter mates. So once you've decided when it will be most convenient to bring a new puppy home, work back these weeks to figure out ideally when your prospective puppy will be, or will have been, born. Ideally you'll want to visit the puppies around the six/ seven-week mark.

When to start looking

Many breeders advertise litters as soon as the mother is pregnant, so it's wise not to leave your search to the last few weeks. If you're looking for a family pet, your search shouldn't take more than a few months. However, if you're looking for a dog that is competition- or breeding-quality you could be looking for up to two years before actually bringing your puppy home. You might be in contact with a breeder before the litter is born, or even before the mother is mated.

But no matter when you start your search, it should begin with identifying the most responsible route to finding puppies for sale in your area.

THE BREEDER

Those first crucial weeks

Choosing the right breeder is one of the most important decisions you will make in choosing your puppy.

The breeder is not only the person who's made the important breeding decisions, he or she is also the person your puppy will spend the crucial first weeks of his life with. I cannot overestimate the significance of the role this person plays in shaping the temperament, character and even behaviour of your puppy.

If you haven't already brought your puppy home, the next chapter, 'Buying Responsibly' is arguably the most important in this book.

4. BUYING RESPONSIBLY

There is an alarming amount of puppy farming going on out there (as well as right here under our noses). Puppy farmers are high-volume breeders who breed puppies with little consideration for the health and wellbeing of the puppies or their parents. They're driven by profit, ignore guidelines on the safe maximum number of litters per dog, and typically separate puppies from their mothers too early. The mothers and puppies live in conditions ranging from substandard to awful, then the puppies are moved to normal-looking homes for viewings – homes which are, in reality, nothing more than a shop front.

So when arranging to see a litter, make sure it's with a responsible breeder. You want to be certain you are buying a healthy, happy puppy and, at the same time, not unknowingly supporting the cruel puppy trade.

Local and online adverts might seem like the obvious place to start your search, but good breeders will be accredited with at least one reputable organisation. Better to start with these:

- the websites of the Kennel Club in your country

  Breeders approved by the Kennel Club (UK) or American Kennel Club (AKC) for example agree to uphold certain welfare standards, to produce puppies in line with the breed standards, and also to reduce or eradicate genetic illnesses.

- Cavalier King Charles Spaniel clubs
- trainers and breeders at dog shows
- dog trainers and behaviour experts
- vets.

Make a list of breeders located close enough to your home for you to be able to visit the litter at least once and pick up your puppy in person.

First contact

Now to make the call. Emailing is of course an option, but you will learn so much more by speaking to the breeder in person. These are some key questions to ask:

- Did you breed the puppies yourself?
  It's imperative they did so you can meet the mother.
- How many puppies are, or were there, in the litter?
  This is to avoid seeing just one puppy. You want to make sure you see all the puppies together so you can compare them and see how they interact.
- If I visit, will I see all the puppies together with their mother and in the place where they were bred?
  This must be a 'yes' and that is where you need to meet the mother as well as the litter.

- For how long have you owned and bred Cavalier King Charles Spaniels?
- Is it only Cavaliers that you breed?

  Ideally it should only be Cavaliers because multi-breed breeders are more likely to be backyard breeders or puppy farmers.
- Are you registered with the Kennel Club or a member of any breed clubs?

  You might already have checked, but if not, ideally this should be a 'yes'. And be sure to check their answers for yourself after the call.
- How old is the mother? And is this her first litter?

  She should be over two and a half years old, and no more than seven. She should have had no more than four litters in her lifetime, and no more than one litter in the space of a year.
- What will happen to the mother when you've finished breeding with her?

  Ideally she will stay part of her already-loving home.
- How do the parent dogs compare to the Cavalier King Charles Spaniel breed standard?

  If they don't know about the standard, or make light of it, you should stay away.
- Have the puppies or their mother had any health problems?
- What health screening has been done for both parents?

  You want to know if there are any hereditary health problems that could affect the puppies going forward. There is more on this in the next chapter, 'The paperwork'. If the breeder doesn't believe in health testing, stay away.

- At what age do you recommend your puppies leave you for their new homes?

  This should never be before eight weeks.
- How many people interact with the puppies on a daily basis?

  Ideally you want the puppies to be experiencing the comings and goings of a family household.
- Will they have been treated for worms before they leave for their new homes?

  They should have received at least one deworming treatment by then.
- Will they have been given their first vaccinations?

  Vaccination requirements vary from country to country, but initial vaccinations generally comprise two doses with an interval of two to four weeks. The first of these is usually given around eight weeks.
- Will they have they been microchipped?

  This is a tiny chip injected under your puppy's skin at the back of her neck. It holds her unique number which links to your contact details and, unlike a collar and tag, it stays there for life. In the UK it is law for all puppies to have been microchipped by eight weeks of age.
- Do you have the relevant paperwork?

  The breeder must be able to give you a record of any vaccinations as this will need to be seen by the vet, as well as taken to any training classes or boarding kennels. They must also give you the relevant details if your puppy has been microchipped so you can change the contact details to your own. If there are any registration and pedigree certificates, you should be able to see these too, along with any health screening results.

There are a lot of questions to be asked, and you don't want this to come across like an interrogation, but you are taking on a new family member who will hopefully be with you for the next 10-15 years. You will be spending a lot of money, and probably travelling a long distance. These questions needn't all be answered in the first call, but they **are** legitimate, and a good breeder will be understanding – appreciative even.

A good and responsible breeder:

- will be happy to answer all your questions on the phone.
- will ask questions of you, to make sure their puppies are going to excellent homes.
- will have photos and possibly video clips of the puppies' parents, and be happy to send you more if you feel you need them (especially if a visit means a lengthy journey on your part).
- will give you the impression of actively loving and nurturing each pup, as well as the mother, to make sure they are well socialised.
- will be happy to arrange a time for you to visit the puppies and their mother in the place where they were born and raised.
- will be happy for you to have more than one visit before pick-up if you feel you need it.
- might give you references of people who've bought puppies from them in the past.
- might give you some form of guarantee against genetic illnesses.
- might offer to take the dog back if you can't keep it. Or even include a contract requiring you to contact them first if you should ever need to give it up.

A responsible breeder will NEVER:

- offer to deliver the puppy to you.
- offer to meet you at a random place.
- tell you the mother is out at the vets, or for any other reason. If she isn't there, the puppy most likely wasn't bred there, or there could be a problem with the mother.
- set up the visit so you will see just one puppy. (You should always see the puppies together.)
- tell you the litter has been vaccinated before four weeks of age.
- advise you to take a puppy before at least eight weeks of age.
- suggest that you breed your puppy for money.
- push you for payment.

Adverts

If you have had no luck finding a litter through breed clubs and dog experts, then you could have a look what's advertised on more general 'for sale' sites, but be wary. These are some early puppy-farmer warning signs.

- They often use the same contact number on more than one advert. If the advert is posted on the internet, do a search on the number see if it has been used on any other puppy adverts.
- They often use the same descriptions, word-for-word, in more than one advert. Search a key phrase in the wording to locate duplicate advertising.
- Photos of the puppies or the parents may also have been used on other adverts.

Price

Don't look for a bargain – good and responsibly bred Cavvies aren't cheap. But be just as wary of puppies priced over the average, because silly money can never guarantee you a perfect dog. Don't be fooled by promises of 'free puppy packs' either – they don't necessarily make the seller any more legitimate.

NEVER get a puppy if you have any doubts about the seller or breeder.

Once you've found a breeder you are sure is responsible and caring, and you've identified a litter of puppies you like the look and sound of, and you're as sure as you can be that they're healthy, happy and from a good home environment, set up your visit or visits.

Then find or buy a soft, comfortable cloth or small blanket to take with you. This is so that, if you **do** reserve a puppy, you can leave it with her until you pick her up. It will absorb the smells of her mother and the litter mates until then, and help to make the separation less stressful.

TIP

Let this comfy blanket absorb the smells of you, your house and your family before you go. Put it in the dirty laundry basket for a few hours. That should do the trick!

Then the countdown begins …

… well almost.

5. THE PAPERWORK

First there's the inevitable paperwork to consider.

No paperwork can guarantee how your dog will turn out; all paperwork can be subject to faking; and what's more there's no reason your adorable Cavalier shouldn't be a wonderful and healthy companion without any paperwork at all. But checking the paperwork is an excellent way to minimise the risk!

Most importantly, you want to establish that the breeder has responsibly health checked both the parent dogs before they were mated. If proof can be sent electronically, aim to see as much of it as you can before the first visit.

Health certifications and ratings of the parent dogs

It's important to check health-clearance certificates and ratings for **both** of the litter's parents, even if you don't plan on breeding or competing with your own puppy going forward. Ideally the breeder will have arranged or checked DNA and screening tests for both parents, and calculated the Coefficient of Inbreeding (COI) **before** mating took place.

The recommended tests and checks for the parent dogs differ slightly from country to country, but this will give you a good idea what to look for.

Priority tests (UK):

- Heart disease – especially Mitral Valve Disease (MVD). Should be tested annually
- Eye screening (certified by the BVA, KC, ISDS or ECVO). Should be done annually
- Episodic Falling (EF) – a neurological disease
- Curly Coat/Dry Eye (CC/DE) – disease affecting the skin and eyes.

Recommended tests (UK):

- Chiari-like Malformation/Syringomyelia (CM/SM) – skull disorder affecting the brain and spine
- Coefficient of Inbreeding (COI) – the breed average is 5.5%, but the lower the better (i.e. the lower the percentage, the bigger the gene pool).

Priority tests (US):

- Heart disease (MVD) – Cardiology clearance at 2.5 years old by a board-certified cardiologist
- Annual eye screening – CERF certificate issued by a board-certified veterinary ophthalmologist
- Hip Dysplasia – OFA hip evaluation. The average

total hip score for the breed is 16, but the lower the better. (Scores range from 0-106.)

- Patellar Luxation – affects the stifle joints (knees).

Recommended tests (US):

- Episodic Falling, Curly Coat and Dry Eye (EF, CC and DE) – diseases affecting the brain, skin and eyes
- Syringomyelia/Caudal Occipital Malformation (SM/COM) – skull disorder affecting the brain and spine
- BAER Testing – for inherited deafness.

NOTE: 'Vet checked' is not the same as 'health tested'. The parents must be 'health tested'. The puppies should be 'vet checked'

Health guarantees

Some breeders will supply a guarantee with their pups that covers them against certain inherited health problems.

Vaccination and deworming records

You will need your puppy's own paperwork – to take to your vet as well as to any training classes he might attend or kennels he might need to board at.

Microchipping details

If the puppies have been microchipped, you will need your puppy's individual number and the name of the provider so you can change the existing contact details to your own.

Registration papers (where applicable)

These are the certificates that record your dog's registration number and serve as proof of his ancestry.

You should be able to see them either by email or on your first visit. Ideally they will have been issued by a reputable registry like your national Kennel Club, but beware of smaller, lesser-known registries which sometimes register dogs without proof of pure breeding.

Pedigree documents (where applicable)

These show your dog's family tree and list the breeding decisions that have been made. Pedigree papers are less official than the registration papers because a dog that is registered is always a pedigree, but a pedigree dog is not necessarily registered.

Sales contract

You might also want to see the sales contract that will need to be signed by both parties on pick-up.

6. WHICH PUPPY?

On the day of your visit you'll be itching to get going, but before you set off, remember to take that soft blanket to leave with the puppies in case you do decide to take one of them.

When you arrive, you'll be magnetically drawn to the litter and all well-grounded, sensible thinking will start to disintegrate, but try not to let down your instantly-falling-in-love guard. Not right away.

Basic checks

First try to make sense of the puppies' environment. Is it warm, friendly and homely? You want to be as sure as you can be that this is where they've grown up. Watch how the breeder interacts with the puppies too. Ideally they are being bought up right underfoot and getting lots of human contact. And if you were promised any paperwork, ask to see it.

The mother

Spend some time with the puppies' mother. She **must** be friendly and good-natured if that is what you hope for in your puppy. You should also consider whether she is the actual mother because sadly this does need checking. Does she look like she's just had the litter? And does she interact with her little ones?

The puppies

FINALLY. You can immerse yourself in the writhing bundle of fluffy heart-melters. But keep your wits about you. Study their temperaments and make sure they are:

- happy and confident,
- friendly and interactive,
- and interested in you and everything around them.

And make sure they look healthy?

- They should appear well-fed – no ribs showing, but not pot-bellied either.
- Their coats should be clean and silky, with no bald patches, fleas or ticks.
- Their noses should be clean, cool and damp, and their breathing should be quiet.
- Their eyes should be clear and bright, with no sign of discharge, and they should not be blinking a lot.
- The ears should be clean and not smelly.
- Their gums should be a healthy pink.
- There should be no irritation around the genitals or bottom, or signs of diarrhoea.
- There should be no redness or swelling between the toes on the paws, and they should walk and run with no difficulty.

Which puppy?

All still going well, you can start choosing. But which one? There are no right or wrong puppies, just ones that are more or less suited to you, your family and your other pets. For example, if you already have a dominant dog, a submissive puppy would be a sensible choice. Here are some tips that could help you with your decision:

- Don't rush this. Sit down with the puppies and spend all the time you need with them.
- If you are absolutely sure you want a boy, you could ask the breeder to remove the girls while you meet the boys, or vice versa.
- Play with each one to see how they interact with you. If you play with one then turn away, does it follow you? If not, it is likely to be more independent than a puppy that does.
- Distance yourself and study their energy levels. Some will be more active than others and need more exercise. If you want to walk out lots and play games, choose the busy puppy, and if you lead a quiet life and want cuddles, choose one with a laid-back personality.
- Watch how they interact with their litter mates. This could be an indication of how easy they will be to socialise. For example, if another puppy yelps, do they stop playing quite so roughly? If they play nicely they are more likely to grow into adult dogs that play well with other dogs.
- Sort out which are more dominant and which more submissive. The more dominant puppies will take food and toys from the others, and only seem really

happy when they are on top of the pile while play fighting. More submissive puppies will play happily with their litter mates without trying to dominate. They will allow other dogs to win a toy, or back off when other puppies want the food or a toy. Some puppies are neither, and prefer being on their own.

- Tell the breeder about your family and any other pets, and ask them for their opinion, because they should have experience with the breed and will also have had time to get to know the individual pups.
- Make a noise behind the puppies. Clap your hands for example. If they flinch, that might be a sign of a nervous disposition, and if they don't react, it could be an indication of poor hearing.
- Throw something to see if they run after it, or bring it back.
- As a test, try placing the puppies on their backs and gently resting your fingers on their chests. The puppies that struggle to get free are less patient than the ones that make little effort to get away. You can also do this test by gently lifting the puppies from a standing position, just a foot off the floor and for a few seconds, and keeping them horizontal.

A good choice is an even-tempered puppy with an outgoing nature. But it's often said that you don't choose your dog or puppy, it chooses you, and many people vouch for this. One puppy might spend your entire visit convincing you he's the one you want to take home, and if that's the case, he probably is.

Whichever pup you choose, when you've settled on your choice, that will be the best dog in the world, and time after time you will ask yourself how you got to be so lucky.

Before you leave

(assuming you're coming back for the puppy at a later date)

Identity – If your chosen puppy looks like any of the others, make sure you and the breeder can tell which is yours. For example, the owner might put a coloured collar on your puppy.

Deposit – The breeder will most likely ask for a deposit to secure your puppy. Make sure you get a receipt and a written agreement that the contract is only binding if the puppy is in good health when you collect it.

Sales contract – Confirm with the breeder that they will have a puppy contract ready at the time of collection. This should include details of health screening (for the puppy and its parents); details of the parents; all information to date on vaccinations, deworming, micro-chipping and veterinary visits; and a health guarantee (if applicable).

Food and care – Find out whatever you can about meals. What are the puppies being fed at the moment? How much and how often? Ask to see the food so you can be sure of giving him exactly what he is used to when you bring him home.

Finally, ask the breeder if you can leave your soft puppy blanket with the litter so that when you pick him up, you'll be able to bring all those familiar mummy-puppy smells with him into his new home.

7. PREPARING FOR THE BIG DAY

It almost goes without saying that when you pick up your bundle of joy, and destruction too, you will need buckets of love, oodles of patience and a fantastic sense of humour. But between now and then, you'll also need to do a surprising amount of planning, puppy-proofing and purchasing of paraphernalia …

Things to do

- Arrange a date to pick up your puppy when it has reached the agreed age. While this should never be before eight weeks, if the breeder wants to hold on to the puppies for much longer, it's important that they are socialising them for you during this time. (See 'Socialisation' in Chapter 13). If you will be travelling by car, choose a day when at least one other person can accompany the driver.
- Book a vet visit for about two days after pick up.
- If you will be taking out pet insurance, do your homework now so you can have it in place as soon as you bring your puppy home.
- Puppy proof your home, checking every nook and cranny:
    - Secure the property. This is the most important thing you can do to keep your puppy safe. If you have a garden or yard, ensure the wall or fence is escape proof from the ground up.

- If there is a pool, pond or any deep water she could fall into, fence it off.
- Check that there are no chemicals within reach: pesticides (including slug pellets), weedkillers, fertilisers, etc.
- Consider fitting child locks to bins and low cupboards that might contain these or other potentially dangerous items.
- Cover or hide electricity cables and wires.
- Tie up, secure or pack away anything that could topple over or be pulled by a cord or cable, like a kettle or a heavy bookcase.
- Remove sharp objects and small things she could choke on.
- Be aware of any plants in your house and garden that may be poisonous. It's worth checking online for a comprehensive list, but these are some of the more common varieties: Aloe Vera, Asparagus Fern, Azalea, Castor Bean, Corn Cockle, Crocus, Cyclamen, Daffodil, Holly Berry, Foxglove, Ivy (Hedera Helix), Jade (Crassula Ovata), Jerusalem Cherry, Jessamine, Hyacinth, Lily of the Valley, Milkweed, Mistletoe, Oleander, Philodendron, Rhododendron, Sweet Pea, Tulip, Water Hemlock, Wisteria.
- Also be aware of low lying plants with sharp pointed leaves.
- Remove valuables from the floor.

- Decide on her special place, a suitable comfy space that she can make her own. This is where her crate will be positioned if you choose to use one, or her play pen, or simply her basket and toys. This special place should be somewhere central –

somewhere she can feel safe, but without feeling isolated or excluded. Never a garage or utility room. An ideal position would be against a wall in the room that most of you spend the most time in during the day. If you already have another dog, it should be away from your other dog's special place, at least for starters.

Things to buy, make or borrow

- **Soft blanket** – if you left this with the litter when you chose your puppy, be sure to collect it when you pick her up. Those familiar smells will help make the transition far less stressful.
- **A crate** (also commonly referred to as a cage or den) – this is optional of course, but it would serve as your puppy's own space, a special place where she can be safe, quiet and keep her toys. There is more about this in the next three chapters, but for now choose one that is just big enough for an adult Cavalier to stand up, turn around and lie down in when she is fully grown. (As a guide, a good size crate would measure approximately 76-91cm / 30-36" on the long side.) Wire cages are better ventilated than plastic ones, offer better views, and are easily collapsible.
- **Comfortable dog bed** – this could be a basket, a dog cushion or even a folded blanket, as long as it's soft, comfortable and easily washable. 'Vet-Beds' are a good choice – they're hardwearing and can be put in the washing machine.
- **A harness** – this is a good idea for your puppy when she is learning to walk on the lead because it prevents unnecessary pressure on her throat. It should be a suitable size, adjustable, and

comfortable. The clip for the lead will either be positioned on the puppy's back (which is easy for her to get used to) or at her chests (which is better for training).

- **A collar** – choose one that is soft, lightweight and comfortable. She will soon outgrow it and you can choose a sturdier one then if that's what you prefer.
- **An ID tag** – keep it small and light and have it engraved with her name and your contact details.
- **Short lead** (four to six foot long) – again, nice and light. She's only little.
- **Extendable lead** – these can be dangerous and are not always permitted in parks and conservation areas. That said, used carefully and only once your puppy is used to the short lead, an extendable lead can make walks more enjoyable for you and your puppy.

- **Bowls** – Cavvies have unusually long ears that have the messy habit of dangling into their food and water, so you might want to choose Spaniel-style bowls. These stand higher off the ground and have narrower tops than standard dog bowls. You might also consider a non-spill travel bowl for car trips, and a crate bowl that clips onto the door or side of your puppy's crate so that it can't be overturned. Remember your puppy will be a medium-sized adult dog before long, so consider whether to invest in medium-sized bowls now, or get small bowls for now and upsize in time.
- **Food** – start with the diet your puppy has been on at her breeders. After that you can move her on to the food of your choice. If you are concerned about making the best decision, consult your vet at her first check-up.
- **Treats** – you will need lots of these. They're fantastic motivators when your puppy is first learning the rules, and excellent for reinforcing good behaviour. They should be suitable for puppies and healthy (avoid additives and preservatives, as well as rawhide treats which could get stuck in her throat).
- **A treat pouch** – a handy pocket for loose treats that keeps your own pockets from constantly smelling of dog food. Another option is a small sealable tub that you can shake the treats in noisily to win her attention.
- **Chews** – your puppy will spend around four hours of each day munching on things, so it's up to you to provide what you want her to do this munching on. Chews are essentially long-lasting treats, and make a fabulous alternative to table legs and leather shoes, but with a young puppy avoid any chews

that can splinter. Antler horns are good, and so are Kong toys filled with treats.

- **Toys** – can a puppy have too many toys? I think not. Invest in plenty of toys in all shapes, sizes, textures, colours and smells. She will chew on them, play with them and even snuggle up with them for hours. (It's wise to avoid giving her old shoes because, smart as she is, she's unlikely to differentiate between old and new when she slips inside your shoe closet.)
- **Anti-chew or citronella** – it's worth investing in either of these to spray onto those things she absolutely must not chew on. Expensive chair legs for example.
- **Poo(p) bags** – biodegradable
- **Newspaper** – or equivalent wee-mat material for house-training
- **Carpet cleaner and odour eliminator** – buy these separately or as one product, but make sure it says 'pet friendly'.
- **Hot water bottle** – strong and well covered
- **Grooming kit** – a soft brush or a grooming glove, and a dog shampoo. Don't cheat and use a shampoo for human hair. In time you are also likely to need another brush or comb, blunt-nosed hair scissors, a pair of dog nail clippers, and a dog dental-care kit, but there's no need for any of those right now.
- **Dog gates/baby gates/stair gates** – these are far better than closed doors for keeping a room off-limits. There's a huge choice on the market, but stay away from stretch gates that she could get her head stuck in.

- **Play pen** – this is useful if you are leaving her for a couple of hours because it is big enough for her to sleep, play and poop in if necessary.
- **Car seat, pet travel carrier or dog guard** – if she is likely to be driven around you will need a safe form of restraint. There is more on this in the chapter 'Travelling by car'.

Setting the rules

Before you bring your newest family member into your home, it's essential for you and all the other members of the household to have a serious chat about the rules. Decide among yourselves where your puppy will be allowed, and when. Make sure you are all in agreement about which rooms and pieces of furniture are off-limit. And make sure everyone understands that sneaking her into an off-limit area, or letting her break the rules in any other way, would only be unfair on the puppy in the long run.

If your family agrees that she is not to be allowed on your best chair, it doesn't mean you need to treat her like an underling. You can compromise by making sure she has a place she can call her own – a special bed placed next to the forbidden chair for example.

Choosing a name

You could choose this once your puppy is home, but either way her name is more important than you might think. You will be using it several times a day for years to come so it must be something she will easily recognise.

- Dogs respond better to shorter names – one-syllable names with a hard consonant or consonants like Pip or Zac for example, or two-syllable names such as Bu-ddy or Cor-ky. You might love the name Jezabel or Octavia, but your dog would thank you for calling her Jez or Otto instead.

- Make sure the name you choose doesn't sound too much like a commonly used command: No, Sit, Down, Stay, Come, Here, Good or Fetch. Beau and Jo, for example, sound too much like No.
- And don't choose a name that sounds like that of another member of the household. If your mother is called Anne, don't call puppy Dan; if your cat is Tigger, don't call puppy Digger or Trigger.
- Choose a name that is easy to call out. 'M' and 'n' sounds are soft which makes them more difficult to call out loud than hard consonants like 'p' and 't'. Molly, say, is a less effective pet name than Pippy.
- Never give any dog a name you wouldn't be happy calling out loud in public

8. PICKING UP YOUR PUPPY

The big day has finally arrived. If possible, pick him up early in the day so he can spend lots of time in his new environment before facing his first night without his mother and litter mates.

If you are driving, try to take someone with you to comfort him, but don't take too many people because the journey should be calm and quiet.

Before you go

- If you haven't already set up his special place in a safe but central spot, do that now. Crate or no crate, furnish it with the comfortable dog basket or bed, some toys, and also some treats if you like.
- And if you haven't already sprayed your most valued furniture with anti-chew, now's a very good time.

Things to take

- The remainder of the payment (if necessary)
- An absorbent mat (or similar protection) in case he relieves himself in the car
- Poo bags and cleaning cloths
- Two bowls (one for food and one for water)
- A small amount of food (in a container)
- A bottle of water
- A small selection of toys and chews

- A backup soft blanket or cushion is also a good idea (in case something has happened to the one you left with the breeder)
- A collar or harness and your lead (not extendable)
- A travel crate (if that's your preference) with an item of clothing inside that smells of you.

The big moment

You'll be a bundle of emotions when you arrive – crazy with anticipation, ridiculously excited, slightly nervous and everything in between. That's understandable. This is a big moment! Life is about to change for you, and the world as he knows it is about to change for your puppy. Give him a gentle but gargantuan cuddle, have a play and check that he's still in good health:

- happy, confident and curious,
- that there are no signs of mucus from the nose, bottom or genitals,
- and that his ears are clean and not smelly.

In the excitement

Apart from your new and perfect puppy, don't forget to come away with:

- the blanket you left, if you left one
- the relevant paperwork including:
    - a receipt of payment
    - health records detailing check-ups and procedures, including the vaccination certificate
    - microchip details if relevant (so you can register the puppy under your name).

It's also worth double checking the food type (just in case it's changed), and finding out what times he has been having his meals.

And last but definitely not least, remember to thank the mother as well as the breeder for your beautiful puppy.

Travelling

Make sure your puppy's feeling safe and happy to be with you before you take him away for good. He is totally reliant on you now, so put yourself into those little paws that are being taken away from their mother and litter mates. Realise that he is leaving the only place he has ever known and, if you're driving, getting into a car for the first time too! Ask yourself, "How would I be feeling now?" and "What would I need from this new person or family?" You'd want to feel safe and secure, loved and cherished.

Put his collar or harness on before you set off. This is best done with two people so one of you can hold and distract him while the other puts it on. You don't want it too tight or too loose. You should just be able to put two fingers under the collar, or two fingers between your puppy and the harness at any point.

If you're travelling by car, your puppy would be happiest being held by the passenger in the back seat. He would need to be held securely (legally speaking 'suitably restrained'), so that the driver is not distracted, and be given love and constant reassurance on the journey. However, where you put him in the car will depend on the laws in your country or state, because holding him in the back seat could affect your insurance.

If you've brought a travel crate instead, then arrange the comfy blanket inside, with its scents of mum and the litter mates, as well as the item of clothing that smells of you. Place him gently inside and fasten the seatbelt over the crate. The passenger should sit next to the crate to comfort him. He will probably be too anxious for toys, but offer them anyway.

If the journey home is a long one, you'll need to stop every hour – more if you can. Offer him some of the food and water in the bowls you've brought along, and give him a little walk and the chance to go to the toilet. But always keep him on the lead. Though he's unlikely to stray from you, this would be a terrible place for him to get loose.

Like people, dogs can suffer from travel sickness, so it is possible he might be feeling a little ill or even be sick on the journey.

9. THE HOMECOMING

If you don't already have another dog or other dogs, you might want to skip to the end of these next few bullet points. But if you do, here are some tips on how to introduce them safely and sensibly.

- Stay outside while you introduce them.
  - If possible, arrange for them to meet for the first time away from home. Ideally, choose somewhere your older dog hasn't been before so that the excitement of the new environment will dilute the puppy's presence. Your puppy is unlikely to be protected by her vaccinations at this stage, so try to choose somewhere no other dogs are likely to go.
  - If they do need to meet at home, however, let them meet outside before taking your puppy in.
- Whether they meet at home or away, keep introductions short and sweet to start with, with both dogs on a lead.
- Stand still or walk slowly while they get acquainted, and try not to interfere.
- At home, take your puppy into the house first, before letting the older dog in.
- Lift any pre-existing dog toys and food bowls off the floor for a few days.
- If you already have two other dogs or more, the process is the same but it's imperative that you introduce the puppy to just one at a time.

Whether or not there are other dogs, give her a chance to wee before going inside. Then, when you're ready, carry her into the house and put her in the special place you've created for her, or in her crate (with the door open wide). Sit beside her, arrange the blanket smelling of her mother and litter mates in her bed, and give her a treat.

When she's explored her special place, let her venture into all the areas of the house she will be allowed in, so that she knows this is home. If there are areas of the house that will be off limits to her, then it is better not to let her in there from the start than to change the rules at some later stage. She will be feeling overwhelmed, nervous even, so stay close by her side, a reassuring presence.

All the treats today should be given in her crate or special area – her very own bedroom. Her comfy blanket should stay there and it's advisable to feed her there too. Do everything you can think of to make her feel that this is the best and safest place in the world. If she has a crate and the design is very open, cover it with a blanket leaving gaps she can see out of.

Puppies wee about once an hour and poop several times a day, so take her to a suitable toilet place every hour if you can. She will still piddle and poop wherever and whenever she needs to because she is so little, can't talk to you, and has no idea that in some places this is a no-no. Toilet training is covered in more detail later on, but for now be sure to clean up very well, always using an odour eliminator.

Your puppy needs 18-22 hours' sleep a day at this age, and on this momentous day she is bound to need even more, so try not to overload her senses with too many people or too much excitement. But **your** presence is essential for her peace of mind so, when you're sitting quietly, let her sit with you and sleep on your lap or close by. If your family has agreed that she is not to be allowed on the furniture, then sit on the floor with her in these early days.

Make sure there is always fresh water available to her, and that she knows where it is. Feed her what she is used to and, as far as practical, at the times she is used to. (This is probably three or four evenly-spaced meals a day.) She might not want to eat at first and that's okay, she'll eat when she's ready. Take the food away and re-present it to her a little later.

Aim to give her her last meal of the day a good two hours before her bedtime, so she has a chance to go to the toilet before settling down for her first night.

10. NEW PUPPY SAFETY

Small puppies have no self-control and little in the way of common sense, so now that your puppy's home, the best way to keep him safe is through your and your family's or housemates' own diligence.

- Handle him gently and carry him carefully.
- Keep doors and gates closed and open where necessary.
- Don't shut doors too quickly – your new 'shadow' could be right on your heels.
- Make a habit of looking where you're walking too. He might've been sleeping in the next room just two seconds ago, but that's no reason to assume he's still there now.
- Don't let him play around cars, or even the lawn mower.
- Don't let him near the edges of pools or deep water.
- Be careful with heights too. Don't let him near high balconies, low window ledges, or unsecured staircases.
- Keep electrical cords well out of reach. Apart from shock there is the danger of pulling something down on top of himself (a heavy iron or a boiling kettle).
- Be extra careful with moving or folding furniture such as rocking chairs, recliners and retractable baby or stair gates.

Small children

If you have small children, they must be taught now that he is not a toy.

- They must not be allowed to pick him up without adult supervision.
- They must not be allowed to disturb him if he is sleeping or has taken himself to a quiet place.
- They must leave him alone while he is eating. Meal times should be uninterrupted so there is no need for him to gulp down his food.
- Games should be calm, and if your puppy gets over-excited they should keep still rather than running around squealing.

Other dogs

- If you're worried about your puppy's safety with any existing dogs, use a baby gate or stair gate to separate them in the short term, or put the puppy in his crate or a play pen while the dogs get used to each other.
- Make sure all members of the family give the older dog/s more attention than usual.
- Feed your puppy in his special place for now. Even later, when your dogs are fed together, their eating places should be at least six feet apart.

Cats

When your puppy is this young, he is unlikely to be a problem for your cat. Besides, Cavaliers generally get on well with the family cat, especially if they have grown up with it. But to be on the safe side introduce them with care and expect some lively interaction.

- Keep your puppy on a lead when they first meet, and have a lovely treat ready. If your cat responds by hissing to begin with, your puppy will most likely retreat. But if the cat runs away, be ready to distract the puppy with the treat so he doesn't chase after it.

- If the introduction becomes unpleasant, separate them and try again later. They could be at odds for several weeks until they reach an agreement.
- Always restrain your puppy around the cat until he learns that the cat is not something to be chased.
- Distract him with a toy to teach him that playing with people is more fun than chasing the cat. It's debatable, but that's what we want him to think.
- Don't leave them alone together until you know they can get along.
- If you need to keep your puppy and the cat apart while you're out, use the crate, pen or a stair gate.
- Make sure the cat has safe places high up that it can reach instead of having to run away.

CURIOUS THINGS

Your puppy will be chewing on everything now, using his mouth to find out about the world around him. But there are some 'curiosities' it's particularly important to keep out of his reach:

Non-edibles

- Medication – human medication is the biggest cause of pet poisoning
- Human vitamin supplements
- Anti-freeze and other chemicals – many of these are sweet-tasting
- Paint thinner
- Pesticides, weedkillers and fertilisers
- Toothpaste
- Sponges
- Household cleaners (including toilet cleaners)
- A surprisingly high number of household and garden plants can be poisonous when eaten in large amounts. (See the shortlist and advice in 'Preparing for the big day'.)
- Small metal objects like coins, and nuts and bolts
- Pins, needles and other sharp objects, including spiky low-lying plants.

People food

It's always best to feed your puppy or dog actual puppy or dog food, and simply stay clear of treats from your own plate. But there are some people foods that you must never let him get hold of never mind feed him because, while they are perfectly safe for human consumption, they are poisonous and potentially fatal to dogs. These include:

- Chocolate (especially dark chocolate)
- Xylitol (an artificial sweetener, commonly used in sweets and gum, but also in some sweet foods like low-calorie cake)
- Alcohol
- Onion
- Garlic
- Grapes or raisins
- Avocado.

Also keep dogs away from

- Soft or cooked bones (especially from chicken or pork, as they could get stuck in his throat)
- Macadamia nuts
- Fruit pips or seeds
- Potato peels or green potatoes
- Rhubarb leaves
- Baker's yeast or yeast dough
- Caffeine
- Mushrooms
- Hops (generally in beer).

Dog products

And don't assume everything at a pet shop will be puppy-friendly. Avoid:

- Cow hooves which can splinter
- Raw hide and pigs' ears which can be a choking hazard
- Toys that might become stringy when chewed
- Chew toys made of plastic or soft rubber
- Toys with small parts they could choke on.

Call the vet immediately if you suspect your puppy has eaten something potentially harmful.

Put yourself in your puppy's paws

If you want to be really proactive, put yourself in his itchy paws and busy jaws for just a moment. Being careful not to underestimate his size, determination or intelligence, get down on all fours and examine every nook and cranny to see what temptations call. Then take these away. Get everything out of his reach. Make it as difficult as you can for him to get into any form of danger or trouble.

Then watch over him, just as you would a busy toddler.

11. THE FIRST NIGHT

Crunch time! She's had her supper, a couple of hours ago, and it's time for bed.

Take her outside for a last chance to go to the toilet. Stay with her in the place you'd most like her to go, and be patient. If she goes, make a big fuss of her.

Back inside, make sure her crate or safe space is as appealing as possible, with her comfortable bed and her soft blanket. In the short term, some people make this space in their own bedrooms, setting it up by the side of their beds. Considering the trauma of this first night, to your puppy and yourselves, there is a lot to be said for this. She still wouldn't be able to snuggle up the way she's used to, but at least she could see you and hear you and would know she's not alone.

If her sleeping place is a metal crate, the openness still leaves your puppy quite exposed. So if you've chosen the crate option and haven't already done so, put a blanket over it, making sure she can always see out.

It's a good idea to make a warm, but not too warm, hot water bottle, and wrap it carefully into her comfy blanket. This is to replicate the body warmth of her mother and litter mates when they're snuggled up. You could also put a ticking clock in the bed to mimic a heartbeat. (Another option is comforter toys which offers warmth and a pulsing 'heartbeat', but they're not cheap.) And if the special place is not in your room, consider leaving a radio playing softly to give her the sense she is not alone.

Scatter some toys and treats and make sure she has access to clean water in her non-tip or clip-on bowl.

If the space is big enough to include a place to relieve herself – aside from the bedding and bowls, then cover this with newspaper or an absorbent wee mat.

When crunch time comes, don't fuss over her. Take her collar off if she'll be in a crate, so it can't get caught in the mesh. Then just put her in her crate or special place with a treat, as though she's the luckiest puppy in the world, and close the door: be it a cage door, room door or baby gate.

In all likelihood she will cry at first, but resist the urge to pick her up. If that's where you want her at night, she must learn to stay there from day one. In fact, it's far kinder not to give her any attention when she cries, because any time you 'give in' would just encourage her to cry even harder each time you had to step away again. Be strong for her sake. Know that she is warm, comfortable, fed and tired, and that the cries will soon subside. What's more, she will soon come to like the quiet and safety of her own space.

Your bed or hers?

Where your puppy sleeps is up to you of course – there are plenty of arguments both for and against your bed and we will look at a few of these in the chapter on 'Behaviour' – but here are some reasons why her crate or special area is a good idea, at least to start off with.

- She's not yet potty trained, and accidents in your bed are a great deal more difficult to clean up than accidents in her special place.

- There is the risk of her falling off the bed and getting a fright or even an injury.
- When she is this tiny, there is, albeit small, the danger of rolling onto her during the night.
- Once a dog starts sleeping on your bed, it can be a very difficult habit to break.
- If she is allowed to sleep on your bed now, she's more likely to have separation issues later on.

What about night-time toilet times?

If your puppy is in your bedroom and you hear her shuffling around in the night, get up straight away and take her outside and to the place you'd most like her to go. She's likely to avoid messing in her sleeping place if she can help it.

If she's not in your room, you'll need to set an alarm for the middle of the night so you can get up and take her out. Alternatively, and only if you've laid down a wee mat, you could wait until very early the next morning.

At some stage she won't need this break at all, but whichever option you choose, you'll need to keep this up for the next few weeks at least.

12. THE FIRST WEEK

From just three weeks old your puppy has been socialising and learning to play with his mother and litter mates. Now suddenly he must learn to be with you, and with people, and to figure out a whole new set of rules. He is likely to follow you everywhere. Don't be surprised if he seems nervous, whines, cries, or doesn't want to eat. Give him love and constant reassurance. If he shivers, make him warm and hold him close.

Luckily for you he is at his most impressionable during these early days, so the time and effort you put in now to building a positive relationship will be worth buckets of good behaviour over the months and years to come.

Mesmerizingly cute as he is, your gorgeous bundle of innocence also needs to know his position in the household. For his own sense of security, as well as your relationship going forward, he needs to understand straight away that you are the leader or there will come a time when he will be walking all over you and making the decisions.

We will look at discipline and obedience later on but until you've read that far, if he does something you don't want him to do, don't punish him or show aggression in any form. That would only confuse him and make him fearful.

Instead:

1. distract him
2. encourage him to do something good instead
3. then reward him for listening.

Encourage and reward – praise him at every opportunity for the good things he does in your eyes, so he can begin to learn what is right in your world.

Be clear and consistent in your praise and he will become the most doting and loyal friend you could ever imagine.

Love him

Unconditionally. Do this and the rest will come naturally.

Teach him his name

Use his name to get his attention, and reward him when he responds to it. But be careful not to say it over and over again or he will quickly become de-sensitised to it.

TIP: Never use his name to scold him. It should encourage him to turn his attention to you.

Handle him

Your puppy needs to learn that he is safe with people, that they mean his no harm, and that he has no reason to fear them or react defensively.

He should start learning this straight away through lots of physical contact. Pet him and handle him: fondle his paws, move his legs, run your hand over his tail, feel his ears, touch his nose, gently examine his teeth, rub his tummy, groom him, bath him. Pick him up and carry him around, supporting him at the chest as well as under his bottom.

Keep his special place appealing

Associations with his special place must be positive, so it should NEVER be used for punishment. Make it comfortable and leave toys and treats inside so that it always feels welcoming and homely.

If he has soiled in it, be sure to clean it well.

Encourage him into this space and praise him when he goes in on his own.

Feed and water him

Your puppy should be having three (or maybe four) meals a day at this stage, ideally of the same food he was having with the other puppies in the litter. If you don't know how much to feed him, work out his daily allowance from the instructions on the food packaging. Split this allowance into three or four equal portions and work out a schedule for regular feeding, for example:

- Three feeds: 7am, 12.30pm and 6pm
- Four feeds: 7am, 11am, 3pm and 7pm.

If he's on dry puppy food, you can add a little warm water and let it soak for a minute before feeding him. This makes it easier to eat and digest.

If you have more than one dog, feed them separately – at least six feet apart – to prevent food aggression.

You, or his primary carer if it's not you, should feed him most often. Feed him some of his meal by hand if you like, as this encourages trusting and loyal behaviour going forward.

Water should always be available, and it should be fresh. Don't cheat by just topping it up. Empty the bowl, scrub it clean and refill it every day.

Make sure the last meal of the day is a good two hours before bedtime so he's less likely to mess in the house during the night.

REMINDER
Never let him get hold of anything listed in the chapter: 'New puppy safety'

Manage toilet time

Remember that your puppy needs regular toilet breaks and it's up to you to help him with the when and where.

During the day, take him outside every hour if you can, and lead him to the spot you'd most like him to use. When he does it there, make sure he understands that was a good thing by making a HUGE fuss of him. Give him a treat and tell him what a brilliant, amazing, spectacular dog he is.

At night, he won't want to go to the toilet in his special place but when he is very little he can only hold on for so long, so ideally you should be getting up during the night to take him out, as well as early each morning.

'But what about when he **does** mess inside?' you ask. What of it? He's a baby. Clean up well and be extremely patient. No matter what you've heard or read until now, don't punish him. He won't understand. (There's a whole chapter on toilet training coming up soon.)

Play with him

Spend lots of time playing with him. And encourage him to experience the world through different surfaces. He will be confined to your property until his last vaccinations have taken effect, but you can still introduce him to floor tiles, wood, carpet, grass, sand, rock, soft cushions, paper and blankets. Let him get used to them all.

Give him quiet time

He needs some time on his own too so he can learn not to be anxious later on when you aren't there or able to play with him. (See 'Time alone' in the next chapter.) Shut him in his special place for a few minutes, once or even twice a day. If you have a garden or back yard, let him outside without you, or just with your other dogs, for ten minutes every now and then.

Loosen his collar

If he wears a collar, check the fit every few days. He is growing fast and it'll need to be loosened regularly. You should be able to fit two fingers between the collar and his neck.

Visit the vet

Regulations vary from country to country, so my best advice here is to take his vaccination certificate along to the visit and let your vet advise you on what your puppy needs and when. Most vaccines require several rounds, between six weeks and 16 weeks, so scheme these in during this first visit. And be sure to tell the vet if you have plans to take your puppy to puppy classes or boarding kennels, because either of these are likely to require further inoculation.

Get advice on deworming, and the prevention of parasites.

If your puppy has not already been microchipped, you could have that done now. (In the UK, this is a legal requirement.)

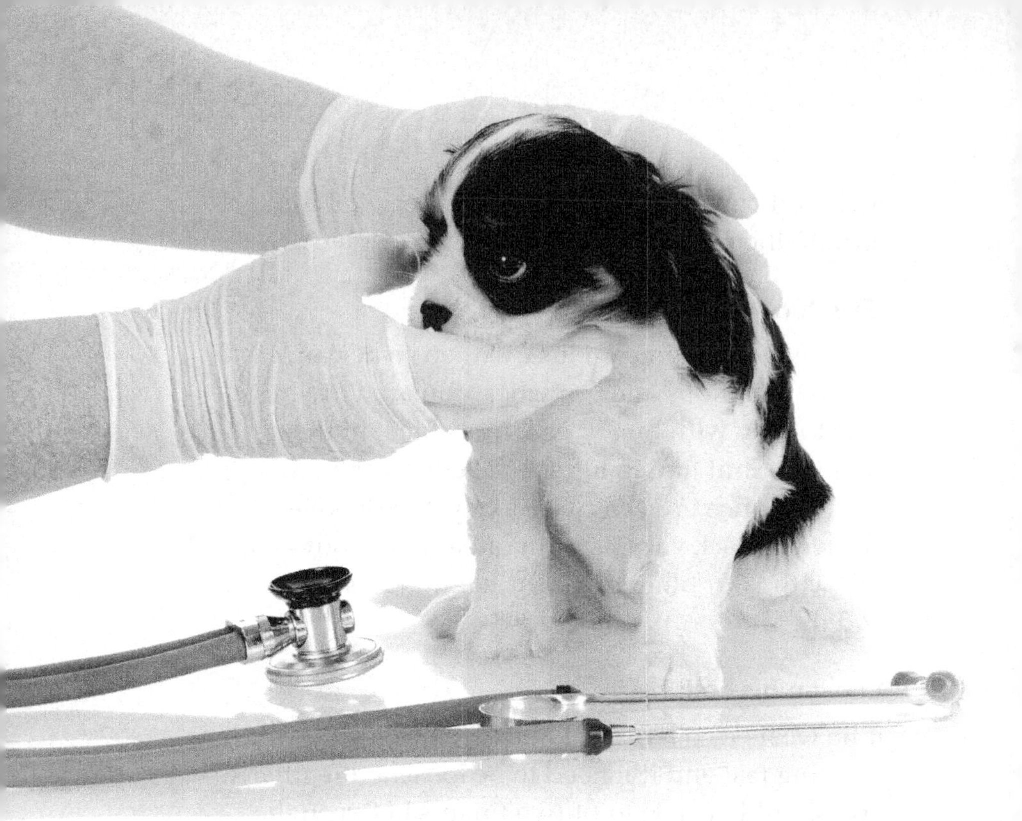

If your puppy's baby nails are very long and catching on everything, you could ask the vet or a veterinary nurse to clip them for you, or to show you how to do it yourself.

Make the visit fun for your puppy by giving him praise and attention, staying by his side when he gets his shots, and telling him how good he is. Possibly take him for a walk or give him a treat afterwards to create a positive association.

Take out insurance

If you're planning on taking out pet insurance, but haven't got round to it yet, do that now.

13. EMOTIONAL DEVELOPMENT

FRAGILE! HANDLE WITH CARE

From eight to approximately 12 weeks is the strongest bonding period you will have with your Cavalier, so it's especially important that you spend it well, giving her lots of time and patience.

She is weaning herself from her mother and you need to be ultra-sensitive to her feelings. Of course, you should always be sensitive to her feelings, but these weeks – known as the 'fear period' – are the very worst time for anything to frighten her. It is a stage when puppies are over-sensitive and when negative stimuli are the most likely to leave a lasting impression. For example, a loud electric storm when your puppy is all alone could lead to a lifelong fear of storms.

But this is also a time of opportunity. It is a particularly good time to show your puppy that most experiences are harmless. And if she's already afraid of something, it's a good time to try to recondition her. For example, if she's afraid of umbrellas, show her that you're not afraid of them by handling them gently in her presence without pressuring her in any way. In fact the more you expose her to the real world now, in a safe and measured way, the more confidence she will have going forward.

SOCIALISATION

In puppy-speak this means introducing her – now while she is still young – to as many people and animals of all shapes, colours and sizes as possible. It is the best way to help your puppy adjust to her new life in your world, and in fact, it is one of the most important things you can do to raise a happy Cavvie. You will be able to teach her fancy tricks for years to come, but during these next few weeks (her vaccination status permitting) it's vital that you get her out and about. Use the time well and don't let it slip by. Visit friends and have friends to visit her. If puppy parties and puppy training are on offer in your area, take her along. (The chapter 'Stepping out' looks at how to do this safely and considerately.)

If you're struck by the bottom sniffling that comes with your puppy's meetings and greetings, you'll soon get used to it. It's how dogs say 'hello', suss each other out and even determine whether they've met before.

HABITUATION

This means exposing her – now while she is still young – to as many new places and conditions as possible. In all fairness, you can't shut her indoors then expect her to behave normally around new people, places and things.

As soon as her vaccinations have taken effect, take her with you everywhere you can and let her explore. Let her discover different smells, surfaces, sounds and sights. Take her into a park, to the school gates, for a walk along a river; go to a sports match, go to the shops, paddle through puddles. Walk her over and under bridges. Let her see cars and trucks and trains and planes. Thunder, lightning and snow might be hard to arrange, but ideally let her experience different weather conditions too. Take her out at night and walk her in the rain.

Feeling safe

It is imperative though that during these new experiences she feels safe as well as having fun. Helping her to feel at ease in new situations will go a long way towards helping her grow up to be a happy and well-adjusted dog, so stay close by her side through these new discoveries and don't let any of them frighten or over-excite her. Going forward, she can only be properly receptive to your training when she is feeling confident and secure.

Here are some ideas to help with this.

- If you come across a potentially frightening situation – some big kids playing rough and tumble at the park for example – watch her closely for signs of discomfort. If she's hiding between your legs, or tucking her tail between her legs, you should back off and find a different route.

- Never put her under pressure to get close to anyone or anything.
- Be alert and sensitive to her feelings so you will know when you can approach and when to stay away. There are many signs which mean different things in different contexts. (See the chapter 'Puppy-People Translator').
- If you're not sure how she feels, avoid having a tight lead so she knows she has a choice. If she is curious, approach from a distance. Let her look, listen and smell, gradually closing the distance as she is comfortable.

Accidental noise

Don't forget about background noises that you are accustomed to, but might be frightening for your puppy.

TV, radio and computers – Be alert to sounds from your devices. Dogs barking aggressively, for example, could leave her terrified. Turn the sound down or off if she becomes alarmed – and before then if possible.

Tension in the house – Keep a good vibe in the house. If she hears angry voices or senses a bad mood, she won't understand that it has nothing to do with her (whether it does or not).

Fireworks and thunder – Close doors and windows, and muffle the sound with your own music or voices. Stay close to her, showing her that you're not afraid.

TIME ALONE

Dog owners are increasingly aware of their dogs' need to be socialised and exposed to everything, and many go to great lengths to arrange this exposure. But just as many owners forget that being alone is one of these experiences. In fact giving your puppy time alone is helping to equip her with one of her most essential life skills.

Cavaliers are highly social and don't like being alone, but most of them **have** to be at some time or another and the best way to minimise or even prevent separation anxiety at a later stage is to start leaving your puppy on her own now, just occasionally, during the day. If she is lucky enough to be right by your side for most of the time this is even more important. Start practicing slowly.

- Choose a time when she is getting tired and likely to sleep soon.
- Take her out for a little play and a toilet break.
- Shut her in her crate or special place with everything she needs.
- Ignore any whining and leave the room or go out for a short while.
- If she is very little and goes to sleep while you are out, open the door or crate door when you return so she can get out when she wakes.
- Start off with about ten minutes and build it up slowly to no more than half an hour at this stage. For one thing, she will soon be needing the toilet.

We will cover time alone in more depth in the chapter, 'Separation anxiety'.

BARKING

It's especially important not to punish barking during your puppy's first weeks in her new home, for all the reasons we've considered. She should be allowed to explore and to express herself.

If she's barking because she's worried about something, and you know her fear is unfounded, lead her away from it and give her a treat when she is quiet. Reassure her with a gentle voice, then gradually expose her to whatever it is that she is afraid of, showing her that you are with her, that you are not afraid and that there is nothing to worry about.

AGGRESSION

This is rarely an issue with Cavaliers, but don't let that lull you into a false sense of security because **any** dog can develop aggressive behaviour. An excellent way to prevent this is by handling your puppy lots and often while she is very young. Teach her now that you can hold and touch her, her toys and her food whenever and however you please. You are the leader and you are in charge.

How? By doing just that. Handle her, her toys and her food whenever and however you please. That way she is less likely to become territorial and possessive over what she considers to be her things.

SMALL CHILDREN

Cavaliers are so good with small children, that it's the puppy that needs protecting from the children, and very seldom the other way round. Put yourself in your puppy's paws and imagine small children rolling around on the ground with you, giggling and shrieking, and how quickly that would encourage you to mouth and nip. Imagine being picked up continually, carried around, possibly even dropped, pestered, woken up … Think what it would be like not to be able to say, 'I don't want to play any more'.

Small children need to learn that your puppy is NOT a toy, and be taught how to behave around her. The following points are reiterated from the chapter 'New puppy safety'.

- They should not be allowed to pick her up without adult supervision.
- They should not be allowed to disturb her if she is sleeping or has taken herself to a quiet place.
- They must leave her alone while she is eating.
- They should not run around squealing, and if the puppy becomes over-excited they should be calm and still.

- They should be allowed to play calm games with the puppy, but nothing involving wrestling or tugging.
- They should sit quietly or stay on their feet while playing, because if they writhe on the ground with the puppy, the puppy is likely to treat them like her litter mates and mouth and bite.

NOTE

Puppies grow up fast compared with human children. One week in your puppy's life is equivalent to around five months' development in a human child.

FURTHER CRATE TRAINING

If you are using a crate and it started off in a temporary position at your bedside overnight, you should move it further from the bedroom – step by step if you like – to its permanent day-time position in the house. But only do this as your puppy grows in confidence and don't rush it. Your job is to build her trust.

If your puppy is going to be in the crate for a lengthy period while you are out, then you should leave her with some food as well as her water and toys, and always keep the area at a comfortable temperature, and free from damp and draughts.

TIPS:

If you want to teach her to like her crate more, try shutting her favourite toy inside for a minute, leaving her on the outside wanting to get in.

Attach a long-lasting chew treat to the inside of the crate – avoiding string she could get tied up in – so that if she wants it, she has to enjoy it right there.

EATING POO – SERIOUSLY?

Your puppy might eat poo – her own or another animal's. But don't panic. Revolting as this is, it's quite common in puppies. It's a difficult issue to address because nobody really knows what it is that makes them do it. The good news is that they pretty much always grow out of it, and quite quickly too.

You might have read or heard advice about upping her vitamin B content, but **never** give her human vitamins. Honestly, apart from sitting it out, the best things you can do are:

- make sure her diet is nutritionally complete
- clean up as soon as she's pooped
- keep her stocked up with interesting chew toys so she doesn't get bored
- keep her on a leash on walks so you can pull her away from other animals' poops
- if you have a cat litter box in the house, move it to somewhere the cat reach but she can't, like on top of the washing machine.

LEADERSHIP

For her mental health and emotional wellbeing, your puppy needs to see you, and all her human family, as her strong, clear leaders. This is never about punishment, but always about clear and consistent communication that prevents bad behaviour from developing in the first place.

Clear communication leads to mutual understanding, and a better life for your puppy as well as everyone else in the family. To achieve it, every member of the family and household must consistently use the same set of rules, spoken commands and body language.

In the chapters 'Behaviour' and 'Training' we will look at the key DOs and DON'Ts to help you build a strong foundation for a lifelong relationship based on understanding and respect.

EXERCISE AND PLAYTIME

These too are essential for your puppy's mental and emotional wellbeing. In the chapter on 'Exercise' we will look at how much and how often, and 'Stepping out' is full of advice and tips for safe and enjoyable outings.

Playing is also essential for a well-balanced, confident dog. It will strengthen her relationship with you as well as improving her overall social interaction. In fact playtime is so important that there's a full chapter devoted to this too, with key pointers to help you make every game and every play session a positive experience.

14. ESSENTIAL CARE

When we think about a puppy's practical needs, our first thoughts are probably about food and hygiene, but before we look at those in detail, here are a few less obvious considerations.

Rest time

Puppies just sleep when they want to. Right? Not necessarily. You need to make sure your puppy has the quiet time he needs, especially if your home environment is busy and bustling. He needed 18-22 hours of rest a day when you picked him up, and by around 12 weeks he still needs a good 15 and 18 hours.

Collar

His collar fitting is also easy to forget, but he is growing fast and it'll need to be loosened regularly. Check daily that it is not getting too tight.

Over exercising

Easier said than done with an exuberant puppy, but try to minimise racing up and down stairs and jumping on and off furniture while he's growing, because his bones and joints are still firming up.

Overheating

This is worth a mention here because many dog owners don't realise how common it is for dogs to die from heatstroke, especially in cars. Dogs can't cool down by sweating like we can. Instead they pant, which is far less efficient. They should never be shut in a hot space, or any place which is likely to heat up quickly. And they should always have a ready supply of drinking water.

Dognappers

Considering the high price of puppies, dog theft is something else to be conscious of. Don't leave your puppy unattended outside for example.

FEEDING

When?

If your puppy was on four feeds a day with the breeder, then carry on with this until some time between 12 and 16 weeks when you can cut his meals back to three times a day. Divide his daily food allowance (according to the instructions on the pack) into three portions

instead of four, and alter your schedule for regular feeding to, for example, 7am, 12.30pm and 6pm. Between six and eight months, you can cut feed times back to just morning and evening, dividing the daily allowance by two.

How?

Here are some tips for this key part of his care.

- Feed him the amount stipulated on the packaging in line with his weight and age, and no more.
- You, or his primary caretaker if it's someone else, should be the person who feeds him most often.
- Keep up with some hand feeding for the few first days, or weeks even. It is a good reminder to him that you are the source of his food. This also prevents him from turning into a growler one day when he might feel his food is under threat.
- If you have more than one dog, feed them at least six feet apart.
- To prevent your puppy from becoming a fussy eater, if he doesn't eat his food, take it away after 15 minutes, and don't feed him again until his next scheduled feed.
- Aim to be consistent with meal times.
- Avoid feeding him immediately before or after exercise, and remember to avoid feeding too close to your bedtime so he's less likely to mess during the night.
- If you're eating around the same time as he is, make sure you eat first to remind him that you are at the top of the pecking order.
- Wash his food bowls daily, throwing out any uneaten food.

Change of food

You most likely started your puppy off on the diet he was having with his breeder, and it is just as likely that in time you will want to change his food. If you do, incorporate the new brand slowly, over the course of one to two weeks. For example, for two to three days give him one quarter of the daily allowance of the new food with three quarters of the daily allowance of the old. A few days later make it half of one with half of the other, again for a few days, then increase the new food to three quarters and finally the full meal.

What to feed

There's a baffling array of dog food brands and flavours on the market, so if you're making this decision without the advice of the breeder or your vet, don't skimp. With dog food you generally get what you pay for. Some Cavvies are fussy eaters, so don't buy more than one bag at a time. That way, if he's lost interest in it by the end of the bag you can soon let him try another brand. It's common for dogs to be hugely enthusiastic about a particular food the first few times they try it and then suddenly change their minds. But whatever your puppy feels about mealtimes, it's only right that you shop around for a food he loves.

- Whatever you decide, make sure you choose a food that is appropriate for the breed.
- Make sure this food is also appropriate for his age – puppies need higher levels of protein, calories and nutritional supplements than adult dogs.
- Many breeders recommend a high-quality dry puppy food (kibble), but whatever you decide on, start by looking at the bold wording on the front of

the packs. The words 'premium' and 'natural' are encouraging signs, but legally the words 'complete' and 'balanced' are better promises of high quality. If you're in the US, look for foods endorsed by the AAFCO.

- Most owners feed either dry food, or canned food (which is smellier and more expensive) or a combination of the two.
- Any food that is 'complementary' is not complete or balanced and needs to be supplemented.
- Always check the ingredients too. The main ingredient should be meat or poultry, not corn or grain.
- Avoid artificial colouring, sweeteners, sugars and salt.
- If your puppy is not faring well on commercially produced food, you could try putting him on a freeze-dried died (these are usually high-quality but costly) or a raw diet. Raw diets require a lot of research and work on your part because this is home-prepared food, mostly consisting of raw meat, whole or crushed bones, vegetables, fruits, raw eggs and some diary.

Overfeeding

Cavaliers are prone to obesity as well as heart disease, so it's important not to let them get overweight, at any stage of their lives, and it's especially important not to let your puppy get overweight while he is still growing.

One way to manage this is to count any treats into his daily food intake, making sure these make up no more than 10%. You could pocket some dry food from his pre-measured daily allowance to use as treats and bribes during the day. Alternatively, you could supplement his diet with carefully chosen snacks – carrots or pieces of apple for example – but never feed these to him as scraps from the table.

Begging

The best way to avoid begging is not to let it start in the first place. Make 'people-food' off limits from day one. Those pleading eyes are near impossible to resist, but you absolutely have to be stronger than he is adorable. Never give in to him if he begs at the table, and never feed him from your plate. If begging does become a problem at mealtimes, confine him to another room until it stops.

Eight months and older

Between eight and twelve months you might want to transition your puppy's food to a 'junior' formula before progressing him on to 'adult' food by around a year.

GROOMING

Many Cavaliers love a good swim, a paddle in the mud, or just racing around through the undergrowth, and their coats – their trademark long ears especially – can be magnets for water, mud and random samples of flora. But even if they are super-clean by nature, there's no escaping the fact that this breed is high maintenance when it comes to grooming. Their long coats are double layered – they have a dense undercoat as well as the silky top coat – and they are shedders too, usually shedding all year round. Lots of grooming is part of the deal. Your puppy is going to need regular brushing, ear cleansing, washing, nail trimming and more.

Brushing

Your Cavvie's long adult coat with all its feathering will only be apparent by about a year, and this will need regular brushing to prevent matting. His puppy coat is shorter, and doesn't need quite so much grooming, but the sooner he gets used to being brushed the better.

Once or twice a week would do, but if this is something you enjoy, then brush away. Brush as often as you like because brushing is much more than detangling and de-matting. It strengthens the bond between you; keeps his skin healthy; aerates his coat and helps you to pick up on any lumps, sores or parasites. It's also very good for teaching him to be handled, especially during vet visits.

Start with a brush with soft bristles and brush in the direction of hair growth. Begin at the head, and work towards the tail and down the legs. Have short sessions at first in case he's getting restless.

It's normal for him to want to mouth the brush, so be patient with him and don't give up because you think he doesn't like it. Build the time up slowly and he will soon come to love these sessions.

As he grows, you will need to take extra care to prevent matting where the coat is longest, including between his toes.

Finish a brushing session by wiping his eyes with a warm, damp cloth. If tear stains become a problem, invest in a tear-stain removing solution.

Ears

Cavvies' long dangly earflaps make their ear canals a haven for dirt and bacteria, so get into the habit now of cleaning them regularly, ideally once a week, and checking for infection.

To clean the inside of your puppy's ears use a warm damp cloth, but never go deeper than you can see. And never use cotton buds. From time to time apply an ear cleansing solution as well.

Signs of infection are an unpleasant smell, crusted or dark earwax, redness or inflammation. Other indicators are more-than-usual head shaking, or scratching or rubbing of his ears. If you suspect infection, take him to the vet straight away so you can nip it in the bud. Ear infections should never be left untreated, and early diagnosis and treatment is also the best way to prevent recurrence.

Going forward, the insides of his ears will need trimming or plucking, either by you or a professional groomer, to prevent the build up of dirt.

TIP: After swimming, always dry the insides of his ears

Washing

Unless your puppy rolls in something stinky and unpleasant, try to avoid washing him more than once a month because washing strips away the natural oils that keep his skin and coat healthy.

You can use your own bath (ideally with a non-skid mat) or a washtub.

- Get everything close to hand before you start. You will need a quality dog shampoo – never use people shampoo or conditioner, a sponge or cup, a soft brush, some treats and a towel. Put on old clothes and a good sense of humour, because you will get wet.
- Lift your puppy carefully into the bath or tub, offering lots of praise and treats.

- Being careful to avoid his head and ears, run lukewarm water over him. This could be with a hand-held sprayer or a cup, or you could soak him with a wet sponge.
- Squeeze a drop of shampoo into your palm, smooth it onto his coat and lather (still being careful to avoid his head and ears) then rinse several times, working the shampoo out with your hands. (Some owners put a cotton wool ball in the ears to keep them dry through this stage of the wash, but never push them in with any pressure.)
- Last of all, clean his head, gently washing the earflaps and wiping inside the ears taking extra care not to drip water into the ear canals.
- Wrap him in a towel and rub him gently before lifting him out.
- When his coat is almost dry, give him a little brush.
- Then let him go, but don't let him outside in the cold until he's completely dry.

TIP: If you want him to get used to the hair dryer, wrap him up in a soft towel, with just his nose sticking out. Face him away from the dryer, and blow him through the towel.
NEVER use a hot setting – always cool or slightly warm, and tested on yourself first.

Trimming

A Cavalier's coat should never be trimmed. Even the fluffy feathering on his feet (sometimes referred to as 'slippers') should be left natural. The only area where trimming is considered acceptable for the breed is under the feet, between the pads and the nails. If this hair gets excessively long, it can be cut back with blunt-nosed scissors to stop it from getting matted.

Nails

Your puppy's nails impact directly on how he walks, so they must be kept short. You might find that exercise on pavements and hard ground wears them down naturally, but any time they do get unmanageably long they will need to be trimmed.

Vets and dog groomers can do this for you but if your puppy's nails need doing as often as every month or two, it would pay off in the long run to buy your own dog nail trimming clippers – which are specially designed to prevent over-trimming – and learn to do it yourself.

Clipping is obviously not something you can practice every day, but what you can do often is help your puppy to get used to the idea. Choose times when he is already relaxed, then take hold of his paw and tap his nails gently with the clippers. When he responds calmly, praise him or give him a treat.

The next stage is to hold his paw, parting the hair away, and clasp a nail in the clippers – without making the clip but still showering him with praise when he stays calm. You might want to get someone to hold him for you when you do this.

When you are ready to make the cut you want to avoid the 'quick', which is inside the nail and contains sensitive nerve endings. If the nails are white or light in colour, you should be able to see the pink of the quick quite clearly. If they are dark, however, clip a tiny bit at a time (no more than a millimetre), inspecting after each clip to make sure there is no bleeding.

If necessary, do no more than one or two nails at a time, praising him after each session, then making a note of the ones you've done.

If he has dew claws – the nails on the upper, inner parts of his feet – then don't forget to trim these too. (He might just have them on the front legs, but if he doesn't have them at all, don't worry. Some breeders will have had them removed soon after birth.)

If you want, you can file the nails smooth with an emery board.

Do nail trimming often so that you won't have to cut much off at any one time, and soon your puppy will be comfortable with the process.

Teeth

Cavaliers have a lot of teeth in a short muzzle which makes them susceptible to dental problems. There are plenty of treats on the market that double as dental chews to clean their teeth and keep their gums healthy. Ideally give your puppy one of these a day.

In addition, it's advisable to brush once a week, and for this you will need dog toothbrushes and meat-flavoured pastes. Start by running your finger along his teeth, being sure to touch all of them. Do this often while you are handling him, just as you might stroke his legs or rub his paws. When he sits still and behaves, shower him with praise, treats and hugs.

After about a week with just your finger, begin using the dog finger toothbrush instead, and when he is managing this, add a small dab of dog toothpaste. (Never use human toothpaste.)

Give this a name, like 'toothbrush time', and he will come to learn that this is when he must sit close to you and keep still. Build the length of the brushing time up to two to three minutes, making sure to clean all the teeth.

Fleas and ticks

To prevent ticks and fleas, it's worth using a breed-specific, vet-recommended treatment, but never before he is 12 weeks old.

If your puppy does get fleas, wash him as usual, combing him while wet with a fine-toothed flea comb. After each brush, rinse the comb in hot, soapy water. Then wash his bedding, and clean and vacuum the house thoroughly to get rid of any unhatched eggs.

If you find a tick, don't panic. It happens. But don't just pull it out either. Cover it with petroleum jelly which will suffocate it and force it to release its hold. Wait five minutes, then pluck it off using tweezers or your nails, from as close to the skin as possible to make sure the head doesn't stay behind.

15. BEHAVIOUR

Your puppy loves you so much! She wants to learn from you and please you. But she only knows what her survival instincts tell her, so, to reiterate, it's your job to teach her what is and isn't allowed in your world.
We will look at specific behaviours in the next chapters, but the pointers in this general chapter are fundamental to every one of them.

For a well-behaved puppy, the first thing to understand – as I'm sure you do by now – is that puppies are much more receptive when they have nothing to fear. A fearful puppy will never be totally engaged.

Our understanding of animal behaviour is improving all the time, and it's no longer acceptable to punish dogs, never mind puppies, by shouting, smacking and rubbing their noses in the carpet. This sort of treatment is not just archaic, it's also ineffective and counterproductive. It scares your puppy and puts you in a bad mood. You lose your dog's trust and the spinout of that – into all the other areas of the relationship – is just not worth thinking about. You want your puppy to be happy and optimistic, looking forward to everything, rather than fearing it.

So how do you achieve this? In a nutshell: you gain her trust by focusing on the things she does right. By encouraging good behaviour and rewarding it.

Encourage and reward

Always tell her what you DO want her to do, rather than what you DON'T want her to do. If she's got hold of your new gloves, don't shout and get angry. Calmly distract her with something else, something she IS allowed to chew on. Refocus her on this new and exciting treat or toy, and rescue the gloves. If you don't have anything at hand, then ask her to do something to obey you – even something as simple as a 'Sit!'

Then, when she IS doing something you DO want her to do, say 'Yes' or 'Good puppy' in a happy and positive voice. And if there's a treat at hand, treat her immediately.

***TIP:** If your treat-bribes start losing their appeal, look for better, tastier ones.*

Her feelings are everything

Let's say your puppy bounces up to you with a glint in her eye, a waggle in her tail and a captured, dishevelled bathmat in her mouth. Try not to think about your favourite bathmat which, after all, is just a thing and has no feelings at all! Instead, think about HOW SHE'S FEELING about what she's done. She thinks she's done brilliantly, doesn't she? She wants a medal. Scold her now and you'll really confuse her. Then again, if you praise her, she might keep bringing you bathmat-type presents ad infinitum. So what do you do?

You don't scold or praise. Distract her instead by calling her to you and getting her attention onto something else, a toy perhaps. When she is refocused on the toy, offer her a tempting chew. By then the bathmat should be far from her mind, and you should be able to rescue it. And if it's still fit-for-purpose, remember to hang it up out of her puppy-jaw reach for a few months.

Prevent bad behaviour

- Don't put temptation in her way. If you don't want her eating from your dinner plate, don't leave it lying around, unattended and in easy reach. That would just be setting her up to fail.
- Try to anticipate things that might go wrong. If you think she's about to chase the cat, hold on to her and distract her with a toy. Dangling tablecloths, for example, are begging for trouble. Don't use them until she's older.
- Make sure her basic needs are met: love, food, water, warmth, things to chew on, sleep, play, exercise and exploration. If she has all of these she is far less likely to behave badly in the first place.
- Don't spoil her. Cavvies are easy to spoil, but too much attention, too many treats, or letting her get away with doing whatever she likes, whenever she likes, is not kind or helpful in the long run.

Ignore her when you disapprove

With many bad behaviours, the best way to tell your puppy you don't like what she's doing is to take away something she wants – your attention. So the very best way to discourage bad behaviour is by ignoring her when she's behaving in any way that is not acceptable to you.

- Don't chase after her when she's taken something she shouldn't have.
- don't yell at her when she doesn't come.
- don't push her off if she jumps up on you or others.

Ignore her, and make it as obvious as you can: stop playing, walk away, fold your arms, look away, even leave the room if you can.

You are the leader

To establish a positive relationship, your puppy must understand from the start that, even though you love her to the proverbial moon and back, and you are best friends, your word is law and she must listen to you. And she will, as long as you are a worthy leader and a good teacher.

Here are some key tips and reminders.

- Don't be aggressive towards her. Be gentle but firm.
- Don't go too easy on her either. In the long run that can be as unfair as punishing her.
- Be crystal clear in your instructions. Use single words rather than sentences and try to be consistent in your choice of words. Don't switch between 'Come!' and 'Here!' for example, or 'Walk!' and 'Heel!'
- Keep your tone positive.
- Use body language as well as verbal commands.
- When she does what you want, show her unreservedly how clever she is. Be happy and excited and reward her with praise.

Alpha dog issues and the bed v crate debate

It's highly likely that your puppy, clever as she no doubt is, will soon decide your bed is the most comfortable place in the world, and that cuddling up there, nice and close to you, is the best and safest way to spend the nights. So while we're on leadership, it's worth noting that letting your puppy sleep on your bed could serve to undermine your top place in the pack. In the wild, being able to choose the best sleeping spot, especially when it is high up, is the privilege of the alpha dog, so even if you do decide to let her sleep there, be sure to let her know where she is and isn't allowed.

Rules must be consistent

I know, I know, we've been here before, but this is really important. If one person lets your puppy onto the sofa, it's downright unfair for someone else to reprimand her for being there. Rules will be very confusing if they differ from person to person, so it's really crucial that everyone in your puppy's life understands and teaches what is and what isn't allowed using the same set of rules, spoken commands and body language.

Timing is all-important

It's vital that you teach your puppy with timely signals too – signals that apply to what she is doing AT THAT TIME. If you try to tell her off for something she did two minutes ago, she won't understand what she's done wrong. For example, if she runs off after a cat and then comes back, and you shout at her for chasing the cat as she is coming back, she will think you are shouting at her for coming back and not for chasing the cat. The result? She will be confused and intimidated, and next time she will think twice about coming back. Many well-meaning dog owners make the mistake of misplaced timing – and it's simply unfair.

When to say 'No!' or 'Leave!'

There will be times when you absolutely do need to tell her her behaviour is unacceptable. For example, if she is doing something that could endanger her or cause harm to someone else. This also applies when she brazenly ignores your command because she would rather do something else.

These need to be corrected immediately and here's how.

- Reprimand her straight away. Say 'NO!' or 'LEAVE!' in your emergency voice – a voice that is so much louder and sharper than your usual quiet and calm voice, that it startles her enough to prevent or stop her behaviour. Use this voice sparingly for best effect.
- Block her way with your body, or physically stop her if you need to.
- Then make eye contact and use your voice to get her to focus on you.
- Once you have her attention, praise her for changing her focus.
- 'No' and 'Leave' are never enough on their own because your puppy doesn't know what she's meant to do instead. Always try to give her something else to do or to chew on.

Still struggling?

If you've tried all these things with a bad behaviour, with repeated, clear and consistent communication, and you're still struggling, you can resort to time-out. Shut her in the kitchen, or a similar and safe place (NOT her crate or special place), and leave her for a few minutes – five is acceptable, ten is too long.

Serious behavioural problems

These include incessant barking and destructive chewing. But all problems are caused by something, be it boredom, loneliness, lack of socialisation, lack of training, fear, anxiety or insecurity, being spoilt or badly treated, or even just poor breeding.

With serious problems, it is especially important that you are able to tell the difference between playfulness and aggression. See the chapter 'Puppy-People Translator' for clues on reading the signs. Cavaliers are rarely aggressive, but if your puppy does develop any traits that could endanger you, herself, or any other person or their dog, you should get help from a professional in dog behaviour. And the same goes for any other serious behavioural problem.

The following chapters (right up to 'Training') focus on the specific challenges you are most likely to face with your new puppy, and are filled with tips to help you as you guide her into adolescence and beyond.

16. TOILET TRAINING

All puppies in the Toy Group take longer to toilet or potty train than the average breed. The good news is that Cavaliers really want to please you, they're willing to learn and they're naturally clean dogs who don't want to soil their beds. If they are able to leave their sleeping area to go to the toilet, they will.

In your puppy's first days with you, he will have no idea that his new home is not a public toilet, so this is something you'll need to teach him – with time and patience.

He has a tiny bladder and bowels, so initially you will need to take him outside hourly and show him where to go. When he does go in an acceptable place, and as soon as he has finished his business, it's time to celebrate. Reward! Reward! Reward! That way you will teach him that doing his business in that place means AMAZING things will happen.

Here are some tips and key DOs and DON'Ts to help speed up the process.

Agree on where

Decide as a family or household on the outside patch or area you'd most like him to use for his business, and this is where you should lead him to every toilet time. Cavaliers are extremely tactile, and he will instinctively look for somewhere soft under foot, like a patch of grass. If you're lawn proud you'll soon learn that lawn and piddles are not a good combination, so if there's a suitable place with soft sand or gravel, encourage him to go there instead. (If that doesn't work, there are plenty of piddle-patch repair products on the market.)

Do

- When you bring your puppy inside for the first time, give him a guided tour of the house. The sooner he understands that all this space is living area, the sooner he will stop using it as a toilet.
- Take him to your chosen piddle patch hourly, including as soon as he wakes, and within 15 minutes of finishing a meal.
- Also take him there immediately if you spot any of these tell-tale signs:
  - Sniffing and circling the floor
  - Pacing up and down
  - Looking towards or sitting at the door to the toilet area
  - Scratching the floor.
- Then wait. And wait some more. Stay with him – come rain or shine – watching him all the time.
- You can spur him on with an encouraging command, like 'piddle now' or 'wee time'.
- Wait until he's completely finished before you reward him, or he might only do half his business.
- As soon as he's finished, shower him with praise.

Don't

- Punish him for piddling or pooping inside, as punishing him for something he can't help and doesn't fully understand would only make him nervous and slow his progress.

- Leave him outside (or in a piddle spot) on his own. He will instinctively turn his attention to getting back to you, and when he does get back, he will very likely still need to go.

Tips

- When he goes to the toilet in the house, thoroughly clean the place he's marked and use a pet-safe odour eliminator. This is because next time he goes to the toilet he's likely to choose somewhere he can already smell wee or poop.
- If he has messed inside but on a training mat or piece of newspaper, carry this outside to where you'd like him to go, and weigh it down there with something heavy. The smell will act as a signal to him to do his business there next time.
- If you're taking him outside during the night just pick him up, take him out, put him on his piddle patch and say 'wee time' or whatever words you've chosen. Don't talk to him or fuss over him and if he gets playful, ignore him or it will be difficult for him to settle back down.
- Once your puppy understands that you want him to do his toiletries outside, you could try hanging a bell on a string from the door that leads to outside. He might well learn to jingle it to tell you when he needs to go out.

How long will toilet training take?

Progress obviously varies from puppy to puppy, but it's safe to assume he'll leave the odd surprise for you until he's around six months, and it could take up to a year for him to be accident free.

17. CHEWING HOUSE AND HOME

All dogs chew, especially puppies. They don't have hands, so chewing is how they explore and learn about the world around them. They inspect everything they can with their mouths and teeth.

They also chew because they are teething. By twelve weeks, your Cavvie's adult teeth, a full 42 of them, are waiting to push out those super-sharp baby teeth. It then takes until around 16 weeks for those baby teeth to even start falling out, and the teething process goes on until he is around eight to ten months. Imagine his frustration. That's a lot of weeks of important but uncomfortable chewing to be done, so for the sake of your puppy, your house and your sanity, keep valuables out of reach.

Your puppy will chew on anything he can during this time. Be understanding, and always have an abundant supply of toys and treats at hand that he IS allowed to chew on.

Don't

- Leave valuable and tempting chewables, like shoes, lying on the floor. Puppies are excellent training for untidy owners.
- Leave supposedly less-tempting valuables lying around either. Things like sunglasses, mobile phones and even car keys.
- Encourage sticks. They can splinter and get stuck in his mouth.
- If you find your puppy with something he shouldn't have, don't try to force it away from him. If it's small enough, he might decide to swallow it rather than give it up.
- And certainly don't start a tug-of-war.

Do

- Instead of trying to pull or coax a forbidden object from him, offer him something he **is** allowed to chew on – a replacement item he'll want even more than whatever he's got. As he plays with the forbidden item, hold the new and better offering to his nose and say, 'Leave!', 'Drop!' or 'Off!'.
- When he drops it, you can give him the treat and a pat.
- Make sure you have an abundant supply of tempting puppy treats and toys. (Pet toys are created to appeal to your dog by smell, taste, feel and shape.)
- Keep these temptations close by. You never know when you'll be needing them.
- If you see your puppy approaching something with demolition on his mind, call him with a happy voice. Puppies are easily distracted, and he should

immediately forget what he'd planned to do and come running to you. Reward him for coming and give him something more suitable to get his teeth into.

- If he's got a taste for something that can't be moved, a table leg for example, spray it with a pet-friendly anti-chew, or citronella.
- If you suspect he has eaten something harmful, call the vet immediately.

Chewing is an essential phase in every puppy's development, and it carries on for months. Hang in there because his need to gnaw on everything in sight **will** lessen. It just won't happen overnight.

TEETHING TIPS

• Tie a knot in an old cloth, wet it and put it in the freezer. Then give it to him when it is frozen to ease his sore gums.

• Give him a chilled or frozen carrot to chew on.

18. MOUTHING AND NIPPING

All puppies love to play, and playing for all dogs involves mouthing one another, so it's completely natural for your puppy to want to play bite. She might also bite because she's teething. It's possible that, like many new puppy owners, you don't mind your puppy chewing your hands now, but you soon will. As she gets older, the biting will get harder and involve others too, so it's important that she learns as soon as possible not to use her teeth on people.

Adult dogs are good at controlling the pressure of their jaws, but puppies often make the mistake of biting too hard because they are still learning and practising jaw control. Your puppy has already learned from the other puppies in her litter that biting inhibits play time. If a puppy had bitten one of its litter mates too hard, the hurt puppy would have yelped and stopped playing.

With you too, she will gradually learn to play more gently until she understands not to let her teeth into contact with your skin at all.

Do

- Play with her with a chew toy in your hand. If she bites you and inflicts pain, make a high yelping sound and immediately withdraw your hand. Because this is exactly what would have happened with her litter mates, it will help her to learn that it's okay to nip the chew toy, but not your hand.

- If the biting persists, remove yourself from the game, the room even, just for a few minutes to show her that teeth on skin equals no more playing. It's not a quick fix, but she will gradually make the association.
- Supervise small children. Their tendency when a puppy mouths them is to scream and run around, which only excites and encourages the puppy even more.

Don't

- Shout at her or smack her if she mouths or nips. This can make the biting harder to control.
- Rush her progress. She must learn jaw control gradually and through experience.
- Play rough tug games – they just encourage biting.

19. JUMPING UP

Your adoring puppy will jump up because she's happy to see you, because she loves you, because she wants to lick you all over your face and she can't reach, because she wants you to pet her and play with her. Although she is used to jumping up on her mother and litter mates, she now needs to learn not to jump up on you or other people. You might not mind her jumping up right now while she's little, but when she is fully grown it's a different story.

And don't forget about those muddy paws and sharp claws. Basically, jumping up soon becomes a nuisance and you want to nip it in the bud before it gets out of hand. So if and when she jumps up:

Don't

- reward her
- talk to her
- tell her to get down
- push her away

- shout or yell
- smack her or use physical punishment of any sort.

Do

- Step back so that her paws don't reach you
- Look away from her
- Turn away from her
- Lift your hands away and don't touch her
- After a few seconds, come back to her, and repeat if necessary
- When she has quietened down and stopped jumping, be sure to praise her and reward her.
- Get all the family to do this, and ask regular visitors to help with it too.
- If jumping up on visitors is likely, put her on a lead before opening the door to them.

How does it work?

These methods will eventually teach her that if she jumps up she will get no attention, and that if she keeps her four paws on the ground she will be praised.

20. DIGGING

It's natural for dogs to dig. That's not to say your puppy will because not all Cavaliers do, but if he does it could be for any number of reasons: because it's fun, because he's bursting with excess energy, because he's made an underground discovery of utmost importance, because he's got something top secret to bury …

Remember that he can't differentiate between the compost heap and your newly planted flowerbeds, so don't get cross with him for digging. Instead, try to understand why he's digging, so you can address it effectively.

If his digging is always at the boundary of your garden or yard for example, he could be looking for companionship and trying to get out. Then you would need to approach the issue in two ways: by making absolutely sure your property is still escape-proof, and by addressing the possible loneliness. (See the chapter 'Separation Anxiety'.)

However, if his digging is persistently in the same seemingly random spot, he's probably got scent of something exciting under the ground right there. If this is problematic, your best bet might be to close his access to the area. Keep him away or fence it off for a while.

Luckily though, the most likely reason your puppy will dig is for the pure fun of it. He's fit to bursting with excess energy and has found a happy way to burn it off.

The best response in this case is probably to tire him out. Try increasing his daily exercise. Take longer walks, increase playtimes and distract him with more toys.

Better still, you could embrace his digging. Make it fun.

- Create an area that's just for him. A place where he's allowed to dig to his heart's content. Make or buy him a sandpit if necessary.
- Bury things there for him to find.
- Then, if you find him digging in other places, tell him 'No!' or 'Leave!', refill the holes he has made, and show him again where he can and should dig instead.

SOMETHING TO TRY

If his digging becomes a real problem try making an unpleasant clanging noise. Rattle some coins in a tin or hit a pot with a metal spoon until he associates his digging in that place with this horrible noise.

21. BARKING

Cavaliers are not typically noisy or yappy, and most will bark only when they're triggered by other dogs' barking or a knock at the door. But some are noisy from the start: they will bark for good reason, for no reason, just for fun, to make suggestions or even to make demands.

If your puppy is one of the more 'vocal' Cavs, he will have a range of bark noises, each with its own distinct meaning, and you'll soon learn to tell the difference between them. Some will be sweet or necessary, but others will become increasingly annoying, and these ones need to be nipped in the bud.

Barking at you

As your puppy comes to see that his efforts to win your attention, like jumping up or nipping, are fruitless, he's likely to start replacing these with his latest greatest trick – a demanding bark noise that says: 'I am still here', 'Stop ignoring me', 'Hey, I want some of that too' or 'Come on, let's play.'

Whatever it is, he wants your attention. Don't give it to him. Instead, pull out your now-well-practiced ignoring techniques.

- Look away and turn away
- Don't talk to him
- Lift your hands away and don't touch him

- Leave the room if you can
- But, as always, as soon as he has quietened down, be sure to acknowledge and reward him.

Barking at others

Most Cavaliers will happily welcome visitors to the house. It's no secret they don't make good guard dogs. But before the door is opened, they might well bark to warn you of the new arrival, and that kind of barking is not necessarily something you want to stop or even discourage. Let him bark, just momentarily, then call him back to you and praise him, or distract him with a toy or a treat if you need to.

However, if your puppy is barking at the neighbour's cat – which is more likely at this stage – and you do want him to stop, your instinct is probably to shout at him to keep quiet. But put yourself in his shoes and you will see that if you shout at him while he is barking, he could think you're egging him on, or even coming to help. The result? He will bark even harder.

So with unwanted barking, as with pretty much all bad behaviour, it is more effective to distract him or give him the 'I'm ignoring you now!' treatment.

> ***TIP:*** *If the barking persists, you could try distracting him with a loud noise. Hit a pot with a metal spoon for example. When he has settled down for a few seconds, acknowledge and praise him.*

Barking to communicate a need

Sometimes barking is a genuine plea for help, for example, if something is truly scaring him or he needs to go outside for the toilet. Always ask yourself why he might be barking. Consider what is going on around her at the time and you will soon learn the difference between attention-seeking barks and barks that express a real fear or need.

Problem barking

This is when nuisance barking, which is annoying but intermittent, becomes incessant and unbearable. But problem barking is never without reason. For example, if a puppy is left on his own for long periods, shut in a small space, or trying not to relieve himself inside, he WILL bark. In fact, he will probably howl. And who could blame him? Wherever barking is linked to a genuine need, it is the need that needs addressing, rather than the barking, so try to find out what's setting him off in the first place. The most common causes are loneliness, frustration, boredom or lack of attention, and here are some things you could try.

Do

- Make sure he isn't barking because he feels threatened by anything.
- Take him for longer walks.
- Give him more time to interact with you and other dogs.
- If he's alone (even in another room):
  - move him to a less isolated place
  - arrange more space for him to play in
  - leave more toys for him to play with.
- If he has to be left alone for a long stretch while you are out:
  - arrange for someone to come and walk him or play with him
  - if this will be a regular occurrence, consider getting another dog for company.

Don't

- Leave your puppy alone for a long time without arranging extra care, like a dog walker for example, and definitely not in a small space. It's simply not fair.

(We will look at this in more depth in the next chapter, 'Separation anxiety'.)

Getting serious

If you've been consistent, persistent and patient with his training and he is still barking incessantly and for no apparent reason, you might need extra help. There are methods you can try and products you can buy, but most of them punish barking rather than reinforcing positive behaviour, so it would be better in the long run to consult a dog behaviour expert who can come to your home.

22. SEPARATION ANXIETY

This is the fear of being alone and it is something all Cavalier King Charles Spaniels are susceptible to. It is not normal for them to be alone.

Separation anxiety can show in a host of negative behaviours, including: barking, whining, pacing, digging and scratching, self-licking, destructive chewing, loss of bowel and bladder control, throwing up, refusing to eat or drink, and even desperate excitement at your return. Repeatedly left alone for stretches of four or more hours, a Cavvie will easily suffer from any or many of these, so don't get one if you're going to be out at work all day.

But of course there will be some times when you do have to leave your puppy alone, even for very short stretches. It's inevitable. So let's look at what can be done now, at the puppy stage, to prevent anxiety from developing.

Your puppy will quickly learn when you're about to go out from the indications you give her – like putting on your shoes, fetching your bag or picking up the keys – and the anxiety will start to kick in as soon as she picks up on these signs. She won't want you to leave, so she'll most likely start following you, jumping up on you and seeking your attention in any way she can. You might think it's sweet that she want to be with you, but for her this a very real form of stress which makes it all the more important that you manage leaving her with care and planning.

First steps

Do your leaving-the-house things often and from day one, even when you're not going anywhere – things like picking up your keys, walking outside and coming straight back in again. This will go a long way to helping her cope with your future comings and goings.

It is wise to start leaving her on her own from early on, for just a few minutes a day, so she understands quickly that this is normal and there is nothing to worry about. But before actually going out for the first time, make sure she's had time to really bond with you.

- Then decide on a special place to leave her, in her crate or a playpen for example, and fill it with everything she needs: bedding, water, food, wee mat. Keep the space small and den-like because this will help her to feel safe. (Giving her free rein in a big house would leave her feeling exposed and even more alone.)
- Next include some distraction toys or treats – items that will keep her so engrossed that she forgets to be worried about being alone. Toys filled with slow-release treats are ideal, like a Kong stuffed

with something as wonderfully yummy as it is difficult to get at, or a Lickimat smeared in it. Poached liver or chicken are irresistible, as is peanut butter (but make sure it doesn't contain Xylitol). There's actually a remarkable range of products on the market that double as separation anxiety aids, including:
    - interactive toys that respond to touch with squeaking or even speaking
    - companion toys – stuffed animal toys that mimic the heartbeat and body warmth of another dog
    - pet cams which enable you to monitor your puppy and even flick her treats via an app on your smartphone.
- With her place and distractions planned, choose a time when she's getting tired and likely to sleep soon, after a walk or an exciting playtime for example.
- Make sure she's had a toilet break.
- Put her in her 'den', ignore any whining and leave the room or go out for a short while (five to ten minutes).
- When you get back, don't make an unusually big fuss of her. Be as matter of fact about it as you can.
- If she's asleep when you return, don't disturb her. Quietly open the crate door or puppy gate so she can get out when she wakes.

Lengthening the separation

When you start leaving her for longer periods, do it very, very gradually, building up to no more than an hour until she is around six months. For one thing, she will be needing the toilet.

Leaving her for a long time

Ideally don't do it. But going forward there could be times when you are left with no choice. Here are some ideas to minimise the stress.

- Drop her off with a responsible family member, friend or dog-sitter.
- Ask a neighbour or pay a pet-sitter to come and spend some time with her, or employ a dog walker.
- Take her for a decent walk before you set off. Exercise has a calming effect, and she'll be more likely to have a sleep when you leave.
- Make sure she has everything she needs, including fresh water and plenty of toys.
- Consider the changes in temperature while you're out. For example, you might've left her in a confined space with a lovely window view, but this might also mean she is trapped in glaring sunlight later in the day.
- You could leave soothing music playing in the house. Some soundtracks are created specifically for keeping dogs calm and comforted.
- If it's likely to be dark when you get home, leave a light on.

TIPS

• *Never punish your puppy for misbehaving while you were out.*

• *Make sure all the other members of the household spend time with her too – feeding her, walking her, playing with her and handling her – so she doesn't become overly dependent on one person.*

23. STEPPING OUT

Apart from playing with you or being snuggled up at your side, there's one other thing your Cavalier will want to be doing, and that is exploring the great outdoors. But first, the baby steps …

You can only start walking your puppy out and taking her on outings once she's been fully vaccinated and once she has had some practice walking on the lead at home. Luckily, while you're waiting for her vaccinations to take effect is the ideal time to practise this lead training.

Eventually all that you want is for her to walk nicely by your side on a loose lead, which sounds simple enough. But with her seemingly endless stores of pent-up energy, this is surprisingly difficult for a puppy to learn.

Do

- Start with a collar or a harness and a short, non-extendable lead.
- Attach the lead when she is calm and not resisting you.
- Then let her wander around the house with the lead trailing behind her, but try not to let her chew it.
- The next stage is to pick up the lead and encourage her to walk along beside you.

- When she is walking nicely alongside you, with the lead slack but off the ground, reward her generously with praise and treats.

Don't

- Drag her. That would only make her panic and pull away.
- If she is pulling, don't be pulled along by her. That would teach her that pulling works in her favour. But don't pull back either, or yank on the lead or shout at her. Instead, stop and call her to you. Praise her when she comes, then try again.

When your puppy is ready for her first walks out, these are a few things to consider and be aware of.

Where and when

Think carefully about where you're going to take her and when, so you can avoid frightening or stressful experiences.

- Choose a safe, open space away from busy roads.
- Choose a place where other dog owners are likely to act in a responsible way.
- And think about the best time to go. Perhaps it's too soon for a Saturday morning at the park if there is likely to be a noisy sports match in play.

What to take

As well as your puppy in her collar or harness and the non-extendable lead, you will need:

- Poo(p) bags – more than one
- Treats (ideally in a treat pouch) – so you can reward good behaviour
- Water and a bowl – if there is no clean water where you are going.

Out and about

- Give her time to sniff at things. She will love exploring new scents.
- Use this time to practice good behaviour and commands.
- If something scares her, let her know you are there with her, protecting her, and that she is safe. Resist picking her up unless it's a real threat.
- Walking out comes with its own risks – some obvious and others totally unpredictable. Beware of other animals, dogs included, and be careful what she might find to eat, for example tasty plants that mightn't be safe.

Pooping

If she poops, pick it up with a poo(p) bag and dispose of it at home, or in a public dog waste bin if there is one.

Other dogs

When you come across other dogs on your outings, you could use the opportunity for your puppy to practise her meeting and greeting. But never assume that other people or their dogs are happy to reciprocate. And never let your puppy run up to other dogs unless their walkers have told you it's okay. There are lots of reasons why it might not be. Perhaps the dog is very old; maybe it is injured; in recovery; not good with puppies; or the owner is working on a specific training exercise. Always ask first and from a distance:

1. whether their dog is good with puppies and
2. whether they are happy for your puppy to say 'hello'.

If it is okay for your dogs to meet, stay close by to supervise, and to pre-empt any bad experiences.

Make sure you walk on past some dogs, and people too, so your puppy doesn't take it for granted that she can run up to anyone for a chin- and tail-wag.

Play dates

If your puppy meets another dog she plays especially well with, you could arrange play dates at times that suit you both.

Together time

- Put your phone out of temptation's way and make this quality time with your puppy!
- If you're going somewhere with big open spaces you might prefer to take an extendable lead. But be extra careful because you have far less control with these. And NEVER pull your puppy back with the line. She should come to you when you call her. There is more on this in 'Training'.

Coming off the lead

When your puppy's very young, she's utterly dependent on you, and much more likely to stay close by your side than she will be in a few weeks or months when she's grown in stature and confidence. For this reason, it's advisable to start letting her off the lead as soon as you're comfortable. This should be for very short stretches to start with, and in safe and carefully chosen places – away from traffic, other dogs and any other conceivable dangers.

In the chapter on 'Training' we will look at Recall, which is teaching your puppy to come to you when you call her. Practice this at home before letting her off the lead when you're out and about. Chances are high that she'll stay close by, and you'll soon be able to gauge how much free rein you can safely give her.

24. EXERCISE

Now let's look at how much exercise to give your puppy through his growing up months, as well as when, where and how.

How much?

Although Cavaliers are highly adaptable when it comes to exercise, the Spaniel in them loves running around outdoors with their noses to the ground. So even if your dog seems perfectly happy curled up with you on the sofa, he must still have daily exercise to keep him healthy and happy.

As an adult, your Cavalier will need a good hour's exercise a day, for example two walks of 30 minutes each. But now, and while he is growing, his bones and joints are still firming up so it's important that his exercise is limited.

As a guide, between eight and 12 weeks take him on two walks a day of no more than 10-15 minutes at a time. Then add five minutes to the length of each walk per month of age. On this basis:

- by four months he should be getting 20 minutes of exercise, twice a day.
- by six months he should be getting 30 minutes of exercise twice a day, or you could split this into three sessions of 20 minutes each.
- between nine months and a year, if you want to increase this, then keeping adding five minutes to each session per month of age. And if at any time you find he is bored, destructive or putting on weight, you can increase this still further.

Until he is fully grown, he should not be going on long hikes.

TIP: *As a rule, more shorter walks are better for puppies than fewer longer ones.*

When to exercise

Ideally this should be once early in the day, and then again in the afternoon or evening. Cavvies are creatures of habit and thrive on routine, so choose exercise and playtimes and stick to them as closely as possible. But avoid exercising immediately before or after eating, or within an hour of his bedtime.

TIP: *If you will be walking him in the dark, invest in a high-vis jacket or a collar with flashing lights.*

Walking

This is fantastic, low-impact exercise for you both. Once your puppy is walking nicely on the lead, you can start picking up the pace, gradually working up to a brisker walk and over longer distances.

Remember he is not 'booted' like you, so be mindful of his paws if the ground surface could be either very hot, or cold and icy.

Games and playtime

These also count towards your puppy's daily exercise and are fantastic for mental stimulation. The Sporting dog in Cavvies means they love a challenge, especially retrieving, so if you want to make your puppy very happy, throw some toys for him to chase and fetch. The chapter 'Playtime' is filled with ideas and tips.

Jogging

Nope! Never jog with your puppy because his bones are still forming. When he's fully grown, he might enjoy a short jog with you, but be sure to build up the distance very gradually, and to no more than 2-3km. Cavaliers are not bred to be running partners and they're certainly not made for long distances.

Swimming

Spaniels in general were bred to retrieve game from water as well as land, and many Cavaliers enjoy swimming. But they're not necessarily natural swimmers, so ALWAYS supervise swimming, and don't push your puppy into anything he doesn't want to do.

The exception is if there's a real need for him to learn to swim. Perhaps, for example, you often walk along a riverside. Then, start him somewhere with a gradual incline into the water and go in with him. He might try to walk on the water at first, lifting his front feet right out with each step. If he does this, hold his bottom up so that his front feet stay underwater.

If he walks in on his own, then stops before he loses contact with the bottom, you could support him under his ribcage, keeping him level until he gets the hang of it.

If you have a pool, you must teach him where the shallowest step or exit is and how to get there. You might need to place a few bricks in the pool to create an extra step while he is learning this. Then lift him into this part of the pool with you and show him how to jump out. Gradually he can learn to get back to the step (or exit point) from further away. Always stay right by his side, ready and watching, guarding and guiding.

When he is older you can throw a ball or a stick into the water for him to fetch.

After swim times, dry the insides of his ears gently but well.

> *NOTE: Swimming is more tiring for him than walking or running, so it's up to you to gauge when it's time to stop.*

BUT

All of these activities come with their own risks – some obvious and others totally unpredictable, so here is a shortlist of things to be alert to. This is not meant to have you deprive your puppy or dog of the great outdoors and the exercise he must have; it's just to help you avoid taking chances with his safety.

On land:

- Even if your puppy or dog is usually reliable off the lead, blind trust is still careless. Don't let him loose anywhere near traffic – animals like birds, squirrels and rabbits could lure him away on a merry chase.

- Make sure you know the area well before letting him off the lead – apart from roads, be aware of cliffs, drainage culverts and thin ice.
- Be careful not to let him 'graze' on greenery on walks. Not all tasty plants are safe.
- If you've been in long grass in the summer months, check him for grass seeds after walks, being extra thorough when checking his paws and ears. Grass seeds are arrow-shaped with pointy ends which attach themselves to your dog's fur. They can pierce the skin, cause all manner of irritation and even lead to infection.

In snow:

De-icing products like salt and grit can contain chemicals that are harmful to dogs. So if you walk your Cavalier on roads and pavements that might've been treated, you will need to wash his paws as soon as you get home. Also wash off any ice or snow balls from his legs, ears and tummy, but only use lukewarm water. It should never be hot.

In water:

As a basic rule, if your puppy is swimming take the same precautions with him as you would with a young child.

- Very cold water can cause hypothermia, which could drain him of his strength to swim to land.
- In the sea, stay clear of rough waves, undertows and side currents.
- Rivers are dangerous when they are fast-flowing, eddying or moving towards a waterfall or weir.
- Be especially careful of steep banks – natural drops as well as manmade ones on the edges of ditches and canals. Anything he could not easily get out of.
- If it's a swimming pool he's in, make sure he knows how to get out.
- In the wild, consider the possibility of other animals in the water: alligators, crocs, sharks, snapping turtles.

After the action

After exercise, Cavvies are instantly blissfully happy to just snuggle up on your lap, or lie quietly by your side.

25. TRAINING

You probably think puppy training is about training your puppy – most people do – but in fact it is nearly all about you, learning how to communicate effectively with your newest member of the family.

Training is all about improved communication and understanding, so think of every minute as an investment in a better quality of life for you, your puppy … and everyone she meets.

Everything from the chapter on Behaviour applies to this chapter too because the premise for training is the same. Because your puppy is more engaged when she has nothing to fear, you should train by encouraging and rewarding good behaviour. Always tell her what you DO want her to do, rather than what you DON'T want her to do.

And training should be fun. The best trained dogs wag their tails during training because they are loving the challenge as much as the reward.

Reward-based training

Praise is a great motivator in training Cavaliers because they always want to please you, but it is not always enough on its own and it is now commonly accepted that training with food-motivation, at least at first, has the best results. When your puppy does something right, reward her immediately with a tempting treat, praising her at the same time with 'Yes' or 'Good dog' in a happy, encouraging voice.

In time, you can wean her from the food-based training and she will obey you purely for the fun of the training itself. But even then, you should reward her with treats intermittently.

When to start

Training starts the moment you bring your puppy home. Even if you've signed up for puppy classes at some future date, don't wait. Teach her what you can, little by little, moment by moment, and make it fun. Practice often, and never give up. When she's under six months, keep these sessions really short – to no more than ten minutes at a time.

Who's responsible

Anyone and everyone in your puppy's close and extended family – and all using the same set of rules, spoken commands, hand signals and body language.

Where?

Start training in a quiet place with few distractions. A closed room is infinitely better than a park filled with people, other dogs and new and interesting smells.

What needs to be learned?

By six months old, your puppy should know her name and obey your orders to: 'Come', 'Sit' and 'Down'. She should also have been introduced to 'Stay'.

How?

All commands should be spoken clearly, firmly and with confidence. Lengthen the vowel sounds and make sure the consonants are crisp and clear.

Your voice and treats are key to training your puppy, but don't forget gestures. It might surprise you to learn that most dogs actually respond better to body language than words.

NAME RECOGNITION

One of the first things your puppy needs to learn is to recognise her name. After all, how else will she know that you're communicating with her?

Do

- From a short distance – three or four feet is fine – call her clearly, using her name just once.
- Use a happy, friendly voice.
- Crouch down if you can.
- Open your arms to welcome her (body language is hugely important).
- Make a fuss of her when she gets to you.
- If she doesn't respond, wait a few seconds then call again, still clearly, and still just the once.
- When she does come, praise her lovingly, give her a treat and tell her how brilliantly clever she is.
- Practise this often.

Don't

- Overuse her name or say it repeatedly in quick succession, or she will soon learn to ignore it.

EYE CONTACT

If your puppy's not looking at you, she's probably not listening either. Calling her name will encourage her to look at you and, when she does, you can know she's engaged. She's turning to you to find out what's coming next: will you open the door, take her for a walk, throw the ball? It's excellent that she's turning to you for answers and provision, so make sure you reward her.

CALLING HER TO YOU

If your puppy only knows one command it should be 'Come' or 'Here'. Coming to you when she's called is important for your relationship, and essential for her safety too. Recall is much like the name recognition exercise and now, while she's little, is a very good time to teach it to her because this is when she needs you more than ever for love, food and safety. In fact, if she's already joined your family, chances are she is with you right now, under your feet or helping you to absorb this book. Digest it even. And chances are she already relates the recall command to something fun and exciting: food, a new toy or playtime.

Do

- Follow the steps in the Name Recognition exercise above, using her name and adding a calling word like 'Come' or 'Here'. Consistency is key, so choose whichever word you prefer and stick with it.
- Call her to you often, gradually increasing the initial distance between you.
- Practice at home and on a lead before you let her go when you are out and about.
- When you do let her off the lead away from home, make sure it is in a very safe place. Then practise letting her go and calling her back.

- If she keeps following you anyway, find someone who can help you by holding her while you back away. Then entice her, if necessary, and when she is struggling to get to you, your helper can let her go. Only then, when she is running to you, call her name and 'Come' or 'Here'.
- Your welcoming body language can be very helpful with this too. Open your arms wide to greet her and, if you can, get down on your haunches or even your knees.

Don't

- If you call your puppy to you and she gets side-tracked en route, you might be tempted to scold her when she finally arrives. But coming to you should ALWAYS be associated with good things, so never punish her if she doesn't come straight away. If you do, she'll associate the scolding with the last thing she's done – come to you. Then, understandably from her point of view, next time you call her she might think twice about coming back at all. (See 'Timing is all-important' in the chapter on Behaviour.)
- Don't always put her back on a lead when she comes to you, or she will soon learn that coming means the end of her free-play session. Only put her back on the lead after several recalls.

TIP

If she develops the habit of running up to you but then dancing around just out of your reach, start withholding her treat until AFTER you have a grip on her collar.

'SIT'

This is one of the most useful exercises you can teach your puppy.

- Call her to you and hold a treat, palm facing down, just in front of her nose for her to smell.
- When you've got her interest, slowly take the treat up a couple of inches and over her head (slightly behind and above her eyes).
- When she lowers her bottom, and only then, say 'Sit!' and give her the treat.
- Once she is doing this well, you can move on to the next stage. Wait until her bottom is actually on the floor before you say 'Sit!', and then treat her.
- She will soon learn to associate the word with the action. In time she will sit after you've given the command, and you can teach her to sit for

longer stretches, from further away and during distractions.

'DOWN'

- It is best to start teaching this command when your puppy is already in an attentive Sit.
- Without feeding her the treat in your hand, move your hand, still palm down, from above her nose and towards the floor, between her front paws and close to her body.
- When she lowers her nose and front paws, keeping her bottom on the ground, say 'Down!' in a clear voice and give her the treat.
- When she is doing this well, you can wait until her tummy and all four paws are flat on the floor before you say 'Down!', and only then give her the treat.

'STAY'

This is an essential command for your puppy's safety – or that of any dog that might dash out the front door, across a road, or leap out of the car.

The training involves teaching her to remain in a Sit or Down position for increasingly long times before you reward her.

- Once she is in a 'Sit' or a 'Down', say 'Stay!' in a strong but soothing voice, and combine this with a clear hand signal. Point to the ground just in front of her with your arm straight, your palm flat and your fingers together.
- If she gets up, simply ask for the Sit or Down position again and repeat the 'Stay' command.

- When she has stayed for a few seconds, say 'Good!' (or another 'release' word of your choice) and give her a treat.
- Gradually work up to longer times, but no more than 30 seconds, and step back in increments to increase the distance. (Try not to give her unrealistic goals; the idea is to push her to the limit while letting her succeed.)
- Keep her on a lead when you put this command into practice at the front door or in the car.

What if the training's 'not working'?

If your puppy doesn't do what you've asked (assuming she's not hard of hearing):

- she doesn't understand and needs clearer instructions,
- she needs more practice,
- or she needs a better reason to obey you – like a treat, an even better treat (squares of fresh chicken or liver. Yum!), or higher praise.

EXPANDING ON THE BASICS

Extension exercises

Duration – Once your puppy can do an exercise, like 'Sit' for example, you can gradually ask her to sit for longer periods before treating her.

Distractions – You can slowly increase the distractions too. A 'Sit' when a squirrel is taunting your puppy from a nearby tree is very different from a 'Sit' in a quiet place. Once she's mastered the instruction in a quiet room, start practising it in a busier part of the house, then at the park, and so on.

Distance – In time, you can also begin asking your puppy to 'Sit' from slightly further away from you, but start with just a couple of steps and don't forget the all-important hand signals.

Advanced commands – If you'd like to add to these basic commands, your puppy can go on to learn 'Stand', 'Settle', 'Heel' and many more. There are some excellent obedience training guides on the market, and if training classes are available in your area, they are well worth the effort and your puppy would love you for taking her.

PATIENCE AND UNCONDITIONAL LOVE

Cavaliers are ranked average in terms of breed intelligence, so be patient with your puppy. They can also put on some spectacular displays of selective hearing, so don't judge yourself harshly if she misbehaves. Nobody said this was easy. And if your puppy struggles with any aspect of training, remember she's a Cavvie. She **more** than makes up for it in love and kindness.

26. PLAYTIME!

Playing with your puppy helps with socialisation, improves his communication skills, and contributes towards his mental and physical exercise. Most importantly of all, it's great fun. But whether this play is purely for fun or a more structured exercise, always keep these 'Rules of Play' top of mind.

- Start playtimes when your puppy is being good, so you're not rewarding him for bad behaviour.
- Several short play sessions spread throughout the day are always better than one long one.
- Whatever games you're playing, remember he's only little, so don't overpower him. Aim to match your strength, speed and energy to his own.
- As far as possible, get down low to his level.
- If a toy is involved, avoid hard tugging. It puts pressure on his teeth and encourages more aggressive play. A good way to manage the pressure is to hold the toy by your fingertips.
- When your puppy wins the toy, encourage him back to teach him that playing is more about having fun together than possession.
- If the playing does shift from fun interaction to possession of a toy, then stop for a while.
- Always try to calm the playing down before you stop. It's disappointing stopping a game when it's at its most exciting.
- And always end playtime on a good note. If you've had to stop for a moment, restart the game and end

it when things are quiet and friendly.

- Avoid exciting games just before his bedtime.

For playtime to be great fun, you really just need each other – there's no need for fancy toys or expensive equipment. Sharing a walk, throwing a ball or paddling in the shallows can be the most special times. But if you're still looking to expand your activities, here are some ideas.

GAMES

All puppies have their favourites and you'll soon figure out which ones you play best together.

Chase

This is excellent practice for encouraging your puppy to come to you.

1. Flick a treat across the floor.
2. Let him chase after it.
3. When he comes back for more, make eye contact and praise him.
4. Only then flick another treat across the floor, and so on.

Fetch

This is an extension of Chase, but played outside or in a much bigger space.

1. Throw things for him to fetch: a toy or a ball.
2. Say 'Fetch!' as you throw each item.
3. Once he knows to fetch, start throwing the objects into harder-to-reach places.
4. If this doesn't work, throw more interesting toys or tastier treats.

Catch

You can play this with toys, treats and balls.

1. Start with something light and easy to grab hold of, like a floppy soft toy.
2. Throw it in an arc over his head, so if he stayed in place it would land close to his muzzle.
3. If he misses, try to pick it up before he does and he'll soon learn that if he wants it he must catch it before it hits the ground.
4. When he's learned to catch, you can move on to balls as well. (Later he can progress to frisbees which are even more challenging, but start off with a soft disc.)

Which hand?

1. With your hands behind your back, put a small treat or two in one hand and nothing in the other.
2. Make your hands into fists and bring them in front of you.
3. Let your puppy choose which fist he prefers the smell of.
4. When he's decided which hand he's interested in, and it's the right one, say 'Good!' and open your hand, letting him take the treat.

Treasure hunt

Your puppy will love this! All the Spaniels excel at sniffing things out and relish any opportunity to put their skill to the test. What's more, rooting around for hidden treasure can be played just as well indoors as out.

1. The first time you play, let him watch as you hide a treat (something he can eat), then lead him away and say 'Find'.

2. Once he understands how the game works, you can make sure he can't see you when you hide the treat or a toy. Then lead him into the room or area where it's hidden, say 'Find', and this time he will have to follow your smell. (The first few times you might need to guide him.)

One day, when he is older and fully understands the game, you can make it more difficult by using 'Sit!' and 'Stay!' while you hide the treat, and then by hiding it in more difficult places too.

Obstacle course

1. Turn your passageway or garden into an obstacle course – build small jumps, make tunnels, fill a tea tray with water, arrange boxes to navigate around … anything you can think of that is safe.
2. Guide your puppy through the course and reward him with treats each time he overcomes an obstacle.

TOYS

Your puppy will love his toys no matter what they are. Nevertheless, look for variety when you're choosing. You want to expose him to a range of experiences through objects that roll, bounce or squeak; things that are wonderfully chewy, or simply soft and cuddly.

Then, to keep him interested in his playthings, don't put them all out at once. Only let him play with or chew a few at a time, and rotate them through the week or even the day.

Presumably he'll already have a few simple toys, but here are three ideas to make his playtimes that little bit more interesting and challenging.

The maze

There are a number of 'slow feeders' on the market which are maze-like in design. These were originally intended for dogs who gulp their food down too fast, but they also work brilliantly for brain-training.

- Put a treat or two in the middle of the maze and let your puppy use his paws, nose and tongue to work them out before he can eat them. (Make sure you've chosen one suitable for the breed so she can actually manage this.)

The hollow chew

Hollow toys made of hard rubber are available online and from most pet stores. The Kong is a great example; it comes in a range of sizes and is dishwasher safe. Fill one of these with small dog treats, or even with meat, marmite or peanut butter (as long as it contains no Xylitol). Your puppy will spend hours trying to extract whatever you've filled it up with.

Treat-dispensing balls

There are plenty of treat-dispensing or 'activity' balls on the market in a range of shapes and sizes. Put dry food or treats inside one of these and your puppy will love rolling it around to get the pieces out.

EQUIPMENT

Use your imagination, but make sure whatever you come up with is safe, and well secured where necessary.

- Hay bales can be used as jumps, steps and passageways
- Old tires make fabulous jump hoops
- Children's paddling pools are great fun for playing in as well as cooling off in on hot days
- Look in children's toy stores – tunnels, playhouses and sand boxes will appeal to your puppy too.

27. TRAVELLING BY CAR

Of course your puppy would love nothing more than to stand on the front passenger seat, stick his head out the window and feel the wind in his face, but car travel is not the time for free play. He needs to be restrained so that he can't distract you while you're driving, or injure you or himself if you have to stop quickly. The restraint is also there to keep your insurance valid in the event of an accident.

Ideally you should invest in one of the following, depending on whether you want your puppy to travel on the back seats, or – if your car has a rear door – in the space behind the back seats:

- a seatbelt harness – well-padded and comfortable, that fastens securely into your vehicle's existing seatbelt fitting,
- a crate or cage that is small enough to fit in the back area of your car while also being big enough for your adult dog to sit up and have a stretch in,
- a dog guard – fitted between the back seats of your car and the trunk/boot area.

All of these are available in pet stores and online.

Do

- For everyone's safety, use a dog seatbelt, crate or cage, or dog guard.
- If you are using a seat belt, always attach your dog by his harness, never a collar.

- Whenever you are getting him into the car or letting him out, make sure it is on the pavement side of the road and never the side with the traffic.
- For his own safety, teach him to 'Stay!' in the car until he is given a release command.
- On long journeys, stop regularly to let him relieve himself and stretch his legs. These stops will also help ease any car sickness he might experience.
- If it's a sunny day and he's in a travel crate or strapped in, make sure he's on the shady side of the car. Being stuck in blaring sunlight would hurt him just as much as it would you.

Never

- Allow your puppy or dog on your lap while you're driving. He must always be restrained.
- Allow him on the front passenger seat, especially if an airbag is fitted.
- Tie him in place on the back seat by his collar and lead instead of using a proper seatbelt harness.
- Leave him unattended in a hot or even warm car. Not even for a few minutes. Dog fatalities from heatstroke in cars are frighteningly common.

28. PUPPY-PEOPLE TRANSLATOR

Your dog understands your every word, or so it's said. The point is, your choice of words is very important. Even more important though is **how** you say them. Be clear in your speech and body language and be gentle but firm, patient, loving, encouraging, reassuring.

It is also said that a dog can say more with her tail in just a few seconds than her owner can say in hours. If she's already in your life, you will be familiar with her favourite expressions: 'I am so happy to see you!' and 'You're the best thing that ever happened to me!' In her first days with you, you will no doubt have experienced, 'Your face is like a lovely lolly!' And before long, you could be surprised when she lets you know that: 'Your training is coming along very nicely!'

Yup, a lot of your puppy's body language is really easy to read, but truth be told the signs are not always straightforward. How good are you really at understanding her language and feelings? By way of example, a wagging tail can be a sign of happiness as well as one of aggression, so we need to look at the whole picture, including: how she wags it, what the rest of her body is doing at the time and what else is going on around her.

To help with this, here are some Puppy-People translations:

I love you

- Racing to meet you
- Wagging tail
- Licking
- Whimpering

I'm happy and excited

- Tail wagging fast (but watch out as this can also be a sign of concentration or aggression)
- Racing around
- Whimpering
- Pulling lips back and exposing teeth

Let's play

- Wagging tail vigorously
- Rolling head
- Dashing off and jumping back again
- Jumping in front of you, facing you, front legs splayed out
- Elbows on the ground and bottom in the air
- Bounding leaps and running in circles
- Lying down or rolling over
- Barking intermingled with growls (can be confused with aggression)

What is that I hear? Where is it coming from?

- One paw raised
- Head tilted to the side
- Brow raised
- Ears twitch and nose wiggles
- Mouth may be open and panting

Totally chilled out

- Lying on back with legs flopped out
- Curled in a ball
- Lying down watching you

Feeling submissive

- Rolling over onto back, exposing tummy and genitals
- Tail between legs
- Head dipped or tucked in, ears pinned back

I'm curious, and maybe a little concerned, about something going on out there

- Raised paw

I'm frightened or unhappy

- Tail between legs
- Cowering, or lying down
- Ears twitching back and forth
- Staring ahead at object of fear
- Lying down with paws ahead, looking ahead, ready to run
- Raised hackles (hairs along the top of her back)
- Whining or whimpering
- Looking to you for help

I'm in pain or frightened and want your help

- Looking from you to whatever it is she needs, and then quickly back again
- Whining or whimpering

  This is not manipulation. It's a genuine plea for help. Tell her you're there for her and she can count on you.

Feeling aggressive

- Standing up straight
- Ears pinned back, or sharply forward
- Hackles raised
- Low growl with eyes fixed in a direct stare
- Body tense, ready to attack
- Tail held stiffly, or wagging in stiff, quick, stilted movements
- Barking
- Growling
- Sudden unpredictable bites

I'm warning you

- Snarling or growling
- Baring fangs

Feeling lonely and locating other dogs, or sending out a warning

- Howling
- Baying

I want your attention: 'hello', 'look at me', 'I'm bored'

- Barking directly at you

I'm begging you. Pleeez!

- Whining, with pleading eyes

  Yes, it's a heart-wrenching expression, but don't give in to that endearing face. Your environment will help you to tell the difference between manipulative begging and 'I'm in pain or frightened and need your help'. If you're eating a juicy sausage that she's hoping you'll share, it's fairly safe to assume she's begging.

29. ADOLESCENCE

Around six months, your puppy will begin chewing her relentless path through adolescence which is usually the most difficult period for owners. Her newfound independence and low tolerance for boredom will bring an increased interest in exploring, chewing, digging and all manner of relationship-testing behaviour. Hopefully the solid foundations you've laid in the early weeks and months will make this phase a little less wearing. Remind yourself it is short-lived.

Running off

During adolescence, your puppy's love of exploring will reach new heights and she could start running off. If she does, it's most likely because she (or he) is at the onset of sexual maturity and wants to mate, and if this behaviour persists, prevention is always the better option. At home you will need to keep her inside or in a fully enclosed garden or yard, and while walking out she will need to stay on the lead.

But if she does run off, be sure to praise her when she comes back. Never scold her when she gets to you, because in coming back she is being a good puppy. That way she will want to stay with you, and even if she does run off again, she will always want to return.

Sexual maturity

Somewhere between six months and a year, your little girl will come into season and be overcome with the urge to roam, and your little boy could begin mounting things and showing aggression towards other male dogs.

Both sexes, if un-neutered (meaning they haven't been spayed or castrated) might begin marking their territory by urinating. Basically both sexes will experience hormonal changes that are likely to affect their behaviour, so if you're not considering breeding, you will be faced with the important question of neutering.

NEUTERING

To neuter or not to neuter? While neutering is likely to reduce bad behaviours, your puppy's health and wellbeing are important considerations here. This is, in fact, a highly controversial subject and beyond the parameters of this book. Most vets and breeders consider neutering the more responsible option, but to help you decide here are some of the key pros and cons.

Neutering your female dog

(also referred to as spaying or de-sexing)

Advantages:

- It prevents unwanted pregnancies,
- stops her from coming into season (coming into heat), which involves a period of bleeding approximately every six to eight months, lasting anything from two to four weeks,
- reduces hormone-associated mood swings, including possible anxiety and aggression towards other dogs,
- stops her from trying to escape to find a mate,
- keeps persistent male dogs from pursuing her during her season,
- dispels the need for weeks of lockdown. (A female in season should never be left outdoors unattended, even in a secured area. She must be kept indoors, or on a lead when out),
- reduces territory marking by urinating,
- reduces or eliminates the risk of a number of health problems, including infections of the uterus and ovarian cancer.

Disadvantages:

- It involves major surgery (removing the ovaries and uterus),
- increases the risk of urinary incontinence,
- increases the risk of joint problems,
- increases the risk of obesity,
- might reduce stamina,
- might affect the silky quality of her coat.

Neutering your male dog

(also referred to as castrating or de-sexing)

Advantages:

- It prevents accidental breeding,
- lessens dominance and aggression,
- cuts back on undesirable sexual behaviour, such as inappropriate mounting,
- reduces leg lifting and territorial urine marking,
- lowers the urge to run off after females in season,
- minimises the risk of attack by other males,
- reduces the risk of a number of health problems, including prostate disorders and testicular cancer.

Disadvantages:

- It involves surgery (removal of the testicles),
- increases the risk of obesity,
- increases the risk of a number of health problems including bone cancer,
- increases the risk of joint problems,
- might reduce stamina,
- might affect the silky quality of his coat.

When to neuter

The best age for neutering is also open to debate, and an equally important consideration.

With females, some vets recommend neutering before your puppy's first season, while others argue that she should have had at least one season, or even a litter of puppies. With males, some vets will operate any time from eight weeks, as long as both testicles have descended; some recommend neutering after six months but before nine to help curb dominant male behaviours; and others recommend waiting longer.

That said, there is mounting evidence that neutering too early can result in emotional and behavioural problems, and many recent studies argue for waiting until your puppy/dog is through puberty and has reached physical as well as emotional maturity. Physically this is between 18 months and two years for a Cavalier. Emotional maturity is more difficult to pinpoint, but good indicators are less bounce and reduced chewing.

I'd say wait, if you can, until your little boy is at least 20 months, or your little girl has had two to three seasons. But this is an important consideration that is in no way clear cut so please do your own research, and discuss this with your vet as well as other owners.

Neutering won't automatically solve your puppy issues, either completely or overnight, but it should help improve unwanted behaviours in time.

30. GOING FORWARD

This book sets out to answer the most important early-stage questions on owning a Cavalier King Charles Spaniel puppy. It covers the things you need to know when he is still very young – the things you don't want to get wrong in his vital first months. Now here are a few key things to be aware or reminded of as he blossoms into adulthood.

Fear period

As if adolescence isn't tricky enough, it's possible that between seven and eight months your puppy could experience another fear period. Of course you're unlikely to know for sure, but to be on the safe side, prepare yourself with saint-like gentleness, patience and understanding.

The special place

When your puppy is toilet trained and has stopped eating everything in sight, you will be able to start leaving the door to his crate or special space open. In the meantime, remember to keep praising him when you see him going in there on his own.

Food

It is important to keep a check on your puppy's weight. Looking from the side, his tummy should be higher than his ribcage – if it is level or hanging down, he is overweight and this will be putting unnecessary strain on his joints and organs. It is your job to manage his food intake, so if you notice that his weight is creeping up, immediately cut back on the treats and increase the exercise.

Between eight and twelve months you might want to move him on to a 'junior' food, but don't progress to an 'adult' formula until he is over a year.

Food allergies or intolerances can develop as your puppy matures. If he starts persistently scratching, licking or chewing his legs or paws, or rubbing his face, switching to a low-grain or grain-free diet could help to alleviate the symptoms. If his food bowls are plastic, switching to stainless steel or ceramic has also been said to make a difference.

Exercise

As an adult, your Cavvie should be getting at least an hour's exercise a day – ideally 30 minutes every morning and evening. If he shows signs of boredom, hyperactivity or starts putting on weight, you can increase this.

When he's fully grown, you might want to take him on longer walks or some short runs, and if you do, be sure to build up the distances slowly. Be mindful of his paws too, staying away from long stretches of hard ground and surfaces that might be very hot, or cold and icy. And if you take him swimming, remember that it's more tiring than walking or running, and that it's up to you to call an end to his swim sessions.

Nails

Apart from being uncomfortable, nails that are too long can cause splayed feet and lameness. Some active Cavaliers never need their nails clipped, but most do. You can tell they need a trim if his toes splay apart, or his nails scratch the ground when he's standing upright. Better still, check them as part of his regular grooming routine, clipping or filing tiny bits at every bath time or trimming session.

If your Cavvie has dew claws – the nails on the upper insides of his feet – remember that these need trimming too to prevent them from catching on things or growing into the skin.

Collar

Keep up the checks on his collar, loosening it whenever it becomes too tight.

Fine tuning

At a later stage you might well choose to fine-tune your training, or need to deal with specific behavioural issues that might've arisen. There are some excellent and extremely thorough books on the market.

And if you've got the time and inclination for obedience training, showing classes, agility, or even dancing with dogs – any classes or competitions that challenge him physically and mentally – they are incredibly enriching for both you and your dog, and he would love you all the more for taking him.

31. THERE WILL BE TIMES ...

This book is intended as an easy read to offer you some shortcuts with the theory. But there are NO shortcuts with the practice. The practice needs patience and repetition, encouragement and reward.

Tough times

There will be times when your puppy does all sorts of things you don't want her to. When she's bored and teething, she will set her alligator jaws to work, chomping their happy way through your designer chairs. She will gift you with shredded items of now ex-value, and with random deposits of unidentifiable bodily waste.

She will slop her muddy paws across your cream-coloured carpet, then wait until she's well and truly indoors before shaking off the rest of the mud. She will bark when she has something to say, and whine when she's upset or lonely.

For months, your house will be littered with toys, and the tick-tack of little paws will be under your feet when you go to the fridge, the toilet, the shower and the front door.

There will be many times when you're at your wits' end and you will look at her and think, 'What **have** I got myself into?'

Good times

Well it's this: you have a new family member who will bowl you over with her love, drape her hairy self over your best furniture, pull at your heartstrings with her soft, pleading eyes, and test your sense of humour with her endless antics.

But it's precisely because of the boundless affection, long silky coats, big soft eyes and blundering capers that we love this breed so much. So remember that when you feel your patience running thin, and no matter how often your Cavalier seems like a small child covered in fur, don't try to make her more human. Just as she is, she will give you more love and more fun than you could ever imagine, and there will be many times when you ask yourself, 'How **did** I get so lucky?'

Your family has grown by four furry feet and when you get home, your puppy's button nose, sparkling eyes and wiggle bottom tail wait to greet you, ecstatic to see you. She will melt your heart, bring you buckets of laughs and enrich your life with her eagerness to please and unconditional love.

There will also be plenty of times when she does the things you DO want her to do. Praise her – with attention, treats, toys … it doesn't matter what, as long as it's something she loves.

Taking-her-for-granted times

And last, but definitely not least, there will be times when she just IS – a calm, quiet presence by your side. Those are the times when it will be easiest for you to forget or ignore her, and those are the times when it is most important of all to remind yourself, and her, just how special she is.

32. USEFUL CONTACTS

UNITED KINGDOM

The Kennel Club (for various services including 'Find a puppy', 'Find a rescue dog' and 'Find an Assured Breeder'.) Note: 'Assured Breeder' is not a guarantee of health-tested parents

www.thekennelclub.org.uk

The Cavalier King Charles Spaniel Club

www.thecavalierclub.co.uk

Champdogs.co.uk (for responsible breeders or puppies)

www.champdogs.co.uk/breeds/cavalier-king-charles-spaniel

Cavalier King Charles Spaniel Rescue and Welfare

www.cavalierrescue.co.uk

Bliss Cavalier Rescue

www.blisscavalierrescue.org

Downloadable Puppy Contract from the RSPCA (the UK's Royal Society for the Prevention of Cruelty to Animals)

puppycontract.org.uk

Association of Professional Dog Trainers (UK)

www.apdt.co.uk

UNITED STATES

American Kennel Club (AKC)
www.akc.org

AKC Marketplace (for puppies available from AKC-registered breeders)
marketplace.akc.org/puppies/cavalier-king-charles-spaniel

Cavalier King Charles Spaniel Club
www.ckcsc.org

Cavalier Health
www.cavalierhealth.org

Cavalier Rescue USA
cavalierrescueusa.org

Dog Food Advice
www.dogfoodadvisor.com

Association of Professional Dog Trainers (USA)
www.apdt.com

OTHER

FCI (Fédération Cynologique Internationale) – The World Canine Organisation
www.fci.be/en

INDEX